D0233435

POPULAR MUSIC OF THE TWENTIES

POPULAR MUSIC OF THE TWENTIES

RONALD PEARSALL

DAVID & CHARLES

NEWTON ABBOT LONDON VANCOUVER

ROWMAN AND LITTLEFIELD

TOTOWA, NEW JERSEY

ISBN 0 7153 7036 7
First published in the United States 1976
by ROWMAN AND LITTLEFIELD, Totowa, N.J.

Library of Congress Cataloging in Publication Data
Pearsall, Ronald, 1927-
Popular music of the 1920's.
Bibliography: p.
Includes index.
1. Music, Popular (Songs, etc.)—England—History and criticism.
I. Title.
ML286.5.P5   780'42'0942   75-16497
ISBN 0-87471-747-7

Set in 11 on 13 pt Garamond
and printed in Great Britain
by Redwood Burn Limited Trowbridge
for David & Charles (Publishers) Limited
Brunel House Newton Abbot Devon

Published in Canada
by Douglas David & Charles Limited
1875 Welch Street North Vancouver BC

CONTENTS

INTRODUCTION

IT IS OFTEN forgotten that a boom followed World War I, and, when this ceased, inflation and the problems of restoring a peacetime economy created a mood of uncertainty and pessimism. A nation searched for an answer, bitter that a war which had been won should almost have bankrupted its people. Few manifestations of popular music reflected this—only the restless quest for novelty at almost any price showed anything of the deep malaise.

As the decade drew on, people came to terms with the situation, and the fact that Britain was not the home for heroes which had been anticipated was shrugged aside. There was a polarisation of the classes, but among all there was a deep suspicion of authoritarianism and a cynicism about government. It is easy to understand why the autocratic attitude of the British Broadcasting Company (later Corporation) should have alienated so many people.

The optimism of the first year after the war—before the demobilisation of the armed services threw hundreds of thousands of men on to the market to precipitate one of the evils of the age, unemployment on a massive scale—encouraged popular music to proceed as if the war had never happened. Some forms of popular music had pushed ahead during the war, and the Edwardian musical comedy had continued to assert its box-office appeal. The pre-war novelty from America, ragtime, had accommodated itself in many a wartime revue, an entertainment much frequented by officers on leave.

The Plaza cinema, noted for its fine orchestra
(Wonderful London)

But all media, so far as the mass audience was concerned, were unimportant compared with the cinema, which measured its audiences in millions rather than thousands. The cinema was the prime means of escape from anxiety and depression, and continued to be for almost half a century. This, of course, was the silent cinema, though never has an adjective been more loosely applied, for between three-quarters and four-fifths of all professional musicians found employment in the orchestras of the cinemas. For most of the working people, cinema music was the only live music they heard, and light orchestral pieces such as the overtures 'Poet and Peasant' and 'Zampa', favourites of cinema musicians, made their way into the mass musical consciousness, supplemented by snippets, distorted and mangled, of Beethoven and even Bach.

The cinema habit threw music hall into the doldrums, though it had less effect on musical comedy and revue which were directed at the middle classes who were apt to be bored with the 700 pot-boilers a year that Hollywood was producing.

Unquestionably the most important musical event of the decade was the coming of wireless, which brought all kinds of music to all kinds of people—variety to those who would not have been seen dead in a music hall, and classical music to the masses. It was an age in which music was heard, rather than listened to, on the radio, on gramophone records, in restaurants and in the street. The ex-soldier pushing a gramophone on a perambulator was an only too frequent spectacle.

The squeaking, crackling novelty of twenty years before, the gramophone, had come of age, and, with electrical recording,

The Capitol cinema (Wonderful London)

music could be reproduced with a good deal of fidelity. Dozens
of record companies poured tens of thousands of discs on to the
market, some good, some bad, some indifferent, and novelty
numbers, from bagpipes, whistling, ukelele solos, to consorts of
twelve saxophones, intrigued and infuriated. Tin Pan Alley and
the law of supply and demand triumphed—except in the BBC
where Sir John Reith and his associates were determined to
provide what they thought the public ought to have, not what it
wanted.

Important as the wireless was in promoting all kinds of music
that the BBC considered suitable, it did not wholly reflect the
increasing Americanisation of popular music. This had begun as
long ago as the 1890s when the musical *The Belle of New York*
came to London, and before World War I Irving Berlin's
'Alexander's Ragtime Band' made traditional popular music out
of date almost overnight. American musical comedies such as
No, No, Nanette and *Show Boat* dominated musical theatre in the
1920s, and Broadway spectacular revue often pushed the home-
bred product into the wings.

The visit of the Original Dixieland Jazz Band opened up new
vistas for the young, and, after its 1919 season at the Hammersmith Palais, British dance bands called themselves jazz bands and
prepared to spread the gospel, revelling in the new idiom and
fondly believing that they were playing authentic jazz instead of
what has been described as Mickey Mouse music. The king of
British jazz was Jack Hylton, who enjoyed the same sort of
adulation as film stars, and the anodyne music he and his fellow
bandleaders performed was widely suited to the dances of the
time, which derived from the pre-war American walking dances
such as the Boston and the one-step. The fox-trot and, later, the
quickstep were, with the slowed-down waltz, to dominate the
ballroom, with the Charleston and the Black Bottom as lively
variants for the energetic.

These dances were ideally suited to the night-clubs, dance-clubs,
and dinner dances that mushroomed during the 1920s. Every
restaurant and hotel had its dance band, and when Ambrose
moved to the Mayfair at a personal salary of £10,000 a year he

American spectacular revue often swamped the British product

became the highest-paid bandleader in the world. Both dance band musicians and public equated jazz with syncopation, and only when the occasional American jazz musician or band came over was there any doubt that they were right.

The popularity of dance music meant that many popular songs were written with the twin demands of the gramophone record and the dance floor kept in mind. The best popular songs of the period are often rhythmical and harmonically piquant, and simple. British popular songs were often too clever by half, and their unmemorability is in stark contrast to American products. Only Noel Coward and a few others managed to compete with a

'The wedding of the painted doll', used in the early musical film
Broadway Melody (1929), illustrates the best of American
popular music of the 1920s

host of talented American songwriters from, alphabetically, Milton Ager, composer of 'Ain't she sweet?' to Vincent Youmans, composer of the smash hit 'Tea for two'.

During the decade there was little working-class participation in popular music. Music was provided for the less well-to-do by professional musicians and the industry, and there was no feedback from grass roots except some amateurish sampling in Blackpool where the British publisher and songwriter Lawrence Wright (alias Horatio Nicholls) tried out new tunes. Do-it-yourself music was still practised by brass band musicians and singers in the north of England and elsewhere, but these movements were in decline, and devotees of the brass band looked back longingly at the days thirty years before when there had been 40,000 bands in Britain. The only outburst of truly popular participation music occurred with the community-singing fad, a promotion stunt of the *Daily Express* which snowballed for a few months, and this was thought by folk music enthusiasts to presage a revival of folk music. However, this was not to be; folk music had to wait until the 1950s and skiffle to become a broad-based enthusiasm and not just a hobby of the intelligentsia.

Unquestionably more music was played during the 1920s than throughout the previous history of mankind. A popular song broadcast on the radio could reach a bigger audience in one-night than a music-hall song of the Victorian age could get to in half a century. (By 1926 there were 2 million wireless licence holders.)

Both gramophone companies and the BBC went out of their way to popularise what management thought of as high-class music, and avuncular musical appreciation programmes on radio did their best to persuade listeners that classical music was not as bad as it was made out to be. The Columbia Gramophone Company offered large cash prizes for a completion of Schubert's Unfinished Symphony, which created such a furore amongst musicians that the scheme was hastily dropped, a prize being offered instead for a commemorative symphony for Schubert's centenary. The BBC's attempt to make middlebrows of everybody antagonised many, and no week went by without cries of wrath by

Sir Thomas Beecham and others accusing the BBC of debasing music and of engineering the doom of the live orchestra.

The attempt of the BBC to make classical music popular (and popular music classical by vetoing the more dubious material) was paralleled in the press. The popularisers were everywhere, trying to make good music easy and significant in terms that the uneducated would understand, as in the cinema where the orchestras worked out formulas—a violin meant interior love, a muted trumpet meant exterior love, study was denoted by the use of the French horn, and the idiot was represented by the bassoon. The Victorian idea that if good music was presented to the masses they would eventually eschew the inferior was still very much in the air.

Only when the monopoly of the music-givers was broken in the 1950s was this illusion shattered, and it was proved that the tastes of the mass of the people were worse than even the most pessimistic had thought. The perspicacious could have projected this twenty-five years earlier, when the *Daily Mail* conducted a poll among radio listeners.

Looking back, we can only give thanks that the BBC *was* autocratic and austere, that the nonconformists in its establishment *did* believe in the philosophy of giving the audience what it ought to have, not what it instinctively wanted (a regimen of variety and dance music, as on the American model where commercial radio arrived early). A habit was established of providing a minority audience with good music, to lead after World War II to the formation of the Third Programme.

The BBC did not do much for or against popular music; it was a largely passive filter, permitting the infiltration of the amiable dance music played by bands such as those of the Savoy Hotel (which, because of apparent favouritism, was believed to have a tie-up with the BBC). The record companies poured so much stuff out that it was difficult to discover what was specifically wanted by the consumers. Why did 'The toy drum major', a nothing record from the conveyor belt, sell 956,784 records? There was no computer for this phenomenon to be fed into.

Despite the fall in sheet-music sales, the composer of popular

The 1920s was the age of the flapper as well as radio, cinema and the General Strike. She often made an appearance on sheet music covers

songs could still become rich. There were so many outlets—
wireless, gramophone, revue, what little there was left of music
hall, cinema, and pantomime, which was still very popular and
offered a fine platform for catchy tunes such as 'Yes, we have no
bananas'. But there were so many composers trying to get in on
the act: there were the old fashioned ballad composers churning out
love's old sweet songs, there were the ballad composers trying to
update themselves and using the mannerisms of American dance
music, there were the clever boys trying to write numbers for
intimate revue, there were the bandleaders and dance-band
musicians writing tunes they could try out themselves, and there
were the composers of novelty and variety numbers. In the 1920s
there were 40,000 composers on the books of the Performing
Rights Society.

No popular musical form could be certain of itself. Musical
comedies and operettas inexplicably boomed or flopped, topical revues could grind to a halt after twenty performances with
perhaps £20,000 lost, and only a few entertainment media could
go ahead without casting an envious glance at the incredible
popularity of the cinema, where nothing failed and even an *avant-
garde* German film with sub-titles would have a goggling if
mystified audience (and an orchestra playing 'Zampa').

The 1920s was such a complex decade that it is foolhardy to
define what was typical. It depended largely on whether one was
rich or poor; the wealthy were still enormously so, the great land-
owners still had their thousands of acres, and debutantes 'came
out' at prestigious balls. There were yachts at Cowes, and the
narrow lanes of Mayfair were clogged with Rolls-Royces, Lancias
and Lagondas. The war had ended but there was still fighting in
Asia Minor between the Greeks and the Turks, the Bolsheviks
were advancing into Siberia, and there was a potential flash-point
at Fiume on the Adriatic where D'Annunzio was in occupation
defying the great powers to turf him out. The French, for reasons
best known to themselves, occupied Frankfurt and there was
street-fighting in Berlin.

By and large, the newspapers preferred to concentrate on other
things—on the wedding of Sir Oswald Mosley, attended by two

The energetic dancer, immortalised in bronze and ivory (Sotheby & Co)

kings and a rare sprinkling of aristocrats, giving respectability to the extreme right wing (as Bulldog Drummond was also doing). The much-hated Victorian age was brought to mind when one of its eminent survivors, the Empress Eugénie, died, and, for a touch of fashionable religion, Joan of Arc was made a saint. Suzanne Lenglen became lady lawn tennis champion of the world.

Shrewd commentators made analogies with the past. After the fall of Robespierre Paris went crazy with forced gaiety, and there was a dancing mania that vied with that of the 1920s where dancing the whole night through, an event recaptured in many popular songs, was 'amusing', the favourite catch-word of the time. There were wild parties with themes such as 'come as your dearest enemy', 'come as your opposite', and 'come as your secret self', but probably the most bizarre was the Baby Party at which men and women presented themselves in various stages of infancy and pushed one another round a London square. In a decade that was sexually free, one of the favourite parties was the shadow-graph party. A sheet was hung up at one end of a room from floor to ceiling, and the lights were put out except for one behind the screen. The shadows of two scantily dressed figures, man and woman, made a pantomime of meeting, kissing, making love, and the viewers had to guess the identities of their fellow guests.

The Bright Young Things boasted of their emancipation, their freedom from the conventions that had constricted their parents' lives, but in reality their reactions were predictable. There were more women than men, for a high proportion of eligible bachelors had died in the war, and the flappers were competing on a basic level for those that were left. With this in mind the following cry from the heart can be seen as a token of desperation:

> In greedy haste, on pleasure bent,
> We have no time to think, or feel,
> What need is there for sentiment,
> Now we've invented Sex-Appeal?
>
> We've silken legs and scarlet lips.
> We're young and hungry, wild and free.

Our waists are round about the hips
Our skirts are well above the knee.

We've boyish busts and Eton crops,
We quiver to the saxophone.
Come, dance before the music stops,
And who can bear to be alone?
Come drink your gin, or sniff your 'snow',
Since Youth is brief, and Love has wings,
And Time will tarnish, e'er we know,
The brightness of the Bright Young Things.

The path of popular music of the 1920s was also predictable, determined by what had gone before, musically, socially, and technologically. Laziness and lethargy in Britain had enabled the Americans to push ahead with the gramophone, the disenchantment of the young Edwardians with the complacency of their elders had led to the rapturous reception of ragtime, and the dozy traditionalism of British popular-song composers led to stagnation.

The whole bag of tricks was shaken up with the coming of the talking, and the singing, picture. René Clair called *Gold Diggers of Broadway* and *Broadway Melody*, the first two musical films, 'canned theatre', and maintained that they were only filmed musical comedies and revues. Only? The touring musical-comedy companies packed up their tents like the Arabs and silently crept away. This particular straw was too much for their camels.

CHAPTER ONE

THE CHANGING FACE
OF VARIETY

THE ESSENTIAL SPIRIT that nurtured music hall died in World War I. The prevailing atmosphere of the music hall was optimism, and even the sagas of domestic distress sung in pseudo-Cockney were not meant to be taken as tokens of despair. The uplift songs so beloved by the Victorians had no place in the new world that arose after the war when open, uncomplicated humour was at a discount.

For a long time the music hall had operated without serious opposition, and although middle-class devotees had been persuaded away in the Edwardian period by the saccharine of musical comedy, for the mass of people there was little alternative entertainment offered. The cinema altered that; by 1917 3½ million people were going to the cinema daily, and although as yet there was no song—and there would not be for another decade—there was humour and pathos in abundance, two of the qualities supplied by the music hall.

The gramophone had been struggling to come of age in the years preceding World War I, but after it there were scores of companies producing tens of thousands of records a year, with the popular market kept well in mind and Woolworth's offering 7in discs at 6d each. With so many rivals for the attention of pleasure-seekers, the situation of the music hall in the early 1920s was analogous to that of the cinema in the 1950s faced by the

Marie Lloyd was believed to be immortal, and everyone was shocked when she died in 1922; this photograph was taken near the end of her life

threat of television. The cinema magnates speedily retrenched, but the music-hall proprietors, who had for years had it so good, took longer to appreciate the new conditions and continued to act as they had in the golden days, dispensing huge salaries and indulging in lavish display.

Vesta Tilley in her autobiography (when she was writing from Monte Carlo as Lady de Frece) assigned the decline in the music hall to three causes: the cinema, the dearth of good entertainers, and the prohibition on foreign performers, due to prejudice and the increasing power of the artistes' trade union. The absence of foreigners from the bills did not affect singing or the comedy sketches, but it did affect the complementary acts—the acrobats, the jugglers, and those involved with performing animals, most of whom were Europeans.

The 1920s did produce new stars, such as Gracie Stansfield (later Gracie Fields) and Will Fyffe (1885–1947), with the earlier greats continuing their careers as if the music-hall boards were as sound as ever. Harry Lauder, knighted in 1919 for his work in fund-raising and entertaining troops, was fifty when the decade opened, but he had little to do but stand up and sing his famous numbers such as 'Stop yer ticklin' Jock' and 'Keep right on to the end of the road'. Marie Lloyd, Queen of the Halls, was considered by her fans to be immortal, but in 1922, two days after singing 'It's a bit of a ruin that Cromwell knocked about a bit' in Edmonton, she died. After her funeral more than 100,000 people filed past her grave.

Her contemporaries were either retired or past their best. Harry Tate (1873–1940) was best known for his sketches such as 'Fishing', 'Billiards', and 'Golfing' which anticipate television comedy, and there were new situations involving the telephone and the wireless to provide further material, but for many his humour was too bland. Florrie Ford (1874–1941) still provided 'Hold your hand out, you naughty boy' and 'Oh, oh, Antonio', Billy Merson (1881–1947) continued to wax rich on his 1914 hit, 'The Spaniard that blighted my life', and G. H. Elliott, the 'chocolate-coloured coon', carried on the black-face tradition of Eugene Stratton and G. H. Chirgwin ('the White-eyed Kaffir') who died in 1922.

Many of the giants of the Victorian music hall were still alive, including G. H. McDermott, one of the 'lions comique', and Charles Coborn who had scored a hit in 1886 with 'Two lovely black eyes' and who, astonishingly, survived until 1945. A number of the old-timers, such as Tom Costello (1863–1943), best known for his sentimental song 'Comrades', kept going in pantomime. The vogue for male impersonators continued after the war, with Vesta Tilley (1864–1952) who retired in 1920, and Ella Shields (1879–1952), who sang perhaps the best known of the transvestite ditties, 'Burlington Bertie from Bow'.

It is clear that there was no shortage of talent, but with the im-

The cult of the male impersonator was still strong, though Vesta Tilley retired in 1920

mense salaries demanded by the celebrities there was less money to be invested in rising youngsters, and a high proportion of the stars of music hall of the 1920s who had reached their peak in the Edwardian period were now cashing in on their popularity. Men and women who would have gravitated to the music hall stage went into another form of entertainment in which variety turns occupied a prime place—revue.

Some of the more versatile artistes, realising the decline of the music hall, spread their talents. Gracie Fields was earning more than £600 a week in 1927—£100 at the St James's Theatre for playing a straight role in the play *S.O.S.*, £200 at the Alhambra in music hall, and £300 in cabaret at the Café Royal. On top of that there were the royalties from her gramophone records. Although she considered that her true *métier* was the music hall and the stage, Gracie Fields was attracted to the cinema because of the immense sums of money film-makers paid out; Miss Fields received £40,000 a film.

Even before the war revue had had a powerful impact on the music hall, though it had damaged musical comedy far more. In essence, revue was a revival of early Victorian burlesque, and its audience was a good deal more sophisticated than that of the music hall. Intimate revue had been anticipated by the amateur pierrot group, the Follies, in the 1890s and early 1900s. Heavily facetious and relying on word-play, these concert parties had as one of their specialities the 'potted play', and music hall managements did not hesitate to include the Follies and other groups in their bills, just as they incorporated the Bioscope as an act. Eventually the Bioscope, as the cinema, took one part of their audience; the successors of the Follies took the other.

In 1912 Irving Berlin's ragtime hit 'Everybody's doing it' gave its name to a revue, and later in the year the spectacular American revue *Hullo, Rag-Time!* broke surface. Throughout the war revue made headway, and in 1918 C. B. Cochran took over the London Pavilion, put up lights announcing that it was 'The Centre of the World', and prepared to coax a post-war audience from an addiction to music hall and musical comedy. Cochran reconstructed the Oxford Music Hall in 1921 as the New Oxford Theatre, at a cost of £80,000 and presented a spectacular revue, *League of Notions*, while the managements of the London Palladium and the Victoria Palace also turned their backs on old-fashioned variety in favour of revue. Only the Coliseum, home of epic music hall on the grand scale and fit for all the family, and the Holborn Empire kept faith.

To many, revue was only the old music hall up-dated and made trendy, the various components linked by a theme, and certainly there was a chasm between spectacular revue for a family audience and intimate revue directed at the intelligentsia, where in-group references flew thick and heavy. There was room for everyone in revue, from Gracie Fields who scored hits in *It's a Bargain* and *The Show's the Thing* to Beatrice Lillie, epitome of twenties sophistication. There were some who were aghast at what was expected of them; one grand theatrical lady was offered a role in revue, but declined when she found that she would have to dress up as an old crone and fall off a bicycle.

The two leading managers in revue were C. B. Cochran and André Charlot. Cochran had started his first revue *Odds and Ends* in 1914 on a few hundred pounds; after the war he found himself spending £30,000 on a revue, with £1,200 a week salaries. The revue *Mayfair and Montmartre* lost its leading lady, the show flopped, and Cochran found himself with a loss of £20,000. Charlot backed many spectacular and successful revues, but by the end of the decade he was in serious financial difficulties, and in 1931 the Official Receiver found that Charlot had liabilities of £60,000. The management of Edwardian musical comedies had often been embarrassed by productions that for some reason or other failed to appeal to the paying public; the entrepreneurs of revue inherited the fickleness of the customers.

Revue was torn between making up a package that people

Forces revues and concert parties reflected an interest in these forms. This troupe is from the warship Royal Oak

would buy and self-indulgent cleverness. The level of wit was often fourth-form, or at best undergraduate, and hagiographic reminiscences of the period frequently disguise the awfulness of the material; in fact, it was often as bad as Victorian burlesque. However, the extreme tiresomeness was redeemed by some excellent songs and some splendid performers.

The making of a revue Charlot-style was described by Noel Coward. The names of all the numbers in the revue were printed on separate cards, placed on a desk, and juggled with. Key numbers were, first, the finale of the first half; then all the numbers leading up to the number before the finale, which, said Coward, had to be sure-fire. The second number in the second half was extremely important, for it had to be strong, funny, or spectacular enough to woo the audience, including stragglers from the bar, into believing that the second half was as good as the first. With a rough running order established, technical matters were taken into consideration; the artistes had to have time to change their costumes for the various episodes, and it was inadvisable to have two elaborate sets in sequence on the simple grounds of expediency.

Revue had much in common with musical comedy. Where things were dragging, an interpolated number, not necessarily by the production team, was added. A revue theme was often the thinnest of counterfeits; the lavishly-dressed and staged tableaux that were a feature of spectacular revue had also been characteristic of the musical comedy of Edwardian times. There was one important difference: the revue was presented with pace, the lethargic unwinding of a plot was frowned upon, and as pace was so much in tune with the hectic times it was capitalised on in a development that reached its full flowering in the 1930s—non-stop revue.

The sheer professionalism of the Charlot and Coward revues resulted sometimes in soulless streamlined efficiency, and many theatregoers preferred the bland semi-amateurism of the original Follies and their logical offspring, the Co-optimists, who were seaside pierrots who had made the transition to London and were still somewhat bewildered by it all. Like their predecessors the Co-optimists wore ruffles and skull-caps, and had an avuncular all-purpose compère, Davy Burnaby. They started in 1921 with a

*Ruffles and bobbles, skull-caps and amateurism, were the
hallmarks of the Co-optimists and their contemporaries*

stake of £900, and lasted the decade out. Many of the stalwarts of
British comedy, such as Stanley Holloway and Hermione Baddeley,
started their careers as Co-optimists.

The basic ingredients of the Co-optimists were, as one of the
original members put it, 'three pioneers and two pianners'. The
second piano was asked for by Melville Gideon lest, when he had
accompanied everyone else, he was left without the 'pep' to get
over his own songs. The extra pianist was to carve himself a niche
in 1920s dance music—Jack Hylton.

Informality and rapport with the audience made the Co-
optimists a cult similar to that associated with the *Beyond the Fringe*
team in the early 1960s, and they operated outside the West End
citadels catering for a specialised audience. In 1924 the members
took the Palace Theatre at a rent of £750 a week, and stayed there
a year, but the increasing rentals in theatreland proved prohibitive.

The sketches and spoken business of the Co-optimists are forgotten, but during the decade that they were in operation they
drove a number of popular songs on to the evergreen market,
including 'Coal black mammy' (1921), 'I want somebody' (1924),
'I wonder where my baby is tonight' (1925), the waltz 'Always'

(1926), and 'The moment I saw you' (1930). It is interesting to see that the first three of these numbers were ragtime/jazz songs, evidence of the increasing impact of the United States on British entertainment.

Occasionally the Co-optimists came unstuck. In one of their shows, Gilbert Childs was 'horribly bunkered in a number entitled "The Underworld of London after dark" ' (wrote James Agate) and Stanley Holloway was 'stymied by "The Old Blue Boar" a ballad of unimpeachable banality, fragrant with the dust of ages'. In 1924 Arnold Bennett noted in his diary a bus advertisement for the Co-optimists 'Started in 1920—Going on for ever'; across it was pasted 'Last two weeks of present season'.

Certainly revues were not a licence to print money, even when admission charges could be incredibly expensive. In 1925 tickets for the first night of a Cochran revue were priced at 24s. These were printed 27s in error, and Cochran decided to leave it at that. There was no evidence that the extra 3s cut down the audience, for smart revues were taking the place of opera as the places to be seen on opening nights.

In addition to the fickleness of the public theatre management had to contend with other difficulties. The year 1921 was a troubled one, and all forty theatres in the West End were handicapped by coal stoppages, drought, restricted rail services, maladministration, drink restrictions, and the necessity of high admission charges to counteract inflation and increased rentals. In the circumstances C. B. Cochran's revue *The League of Notions* did well with 357 performances, but a promising burlesque at the Gaiety, *Faust on Toast*, staggered on for only 14 performances. It was put on again, management certain that it had a winner, and clocked up another 20. The revue *Fantasia* was even more unfortunate. The ultimate in flops of 1921, it ran for 9 performances. Again management persevered, and it was retitled *Put and Take*, a popular game of the time, but after 20 performances it lay down and died.

Recruits to revue were beginning to show themselves. *A to Z* at the Prince of Wales starred Gertrude Lawrence and Jack Buchanan, produced a first-rate song in 'And her mother came too' with

George Robey used his talents in all the entertainment media. Few would have recognised him, as here, out of costume

music by Ivor Novello, and ran for 433 performances. One of the doyens of the music hall came out of the cold into revue—George Robey; but *Robey en Casserole* at the Alhambra did very modestly with only 108 performances. Robey was one of those who realised that to preserve his cognomen as the Prime Minister of Mirth he had to change with the times, and hurled himself into all the entertainment media he could—revue, music hall, pantomime, musical comedy, Shakespearian drama, and cinema (he acted in ten silent films from 1914 to 1924, and was in fourteen talkies from 1932 to 1952).

Contemporaneousness was one of the ingredients of the smart revue, and one of the reasons offered for the ghastly failure of *Faust on Toast* was its outmoded literary flavour. In 1922 the wire-

*Cicely Courtneidge was one of the finds of the
1920s achieving fame as a light comedienne and
not as a pin-up*

less was beginning to make headway, with 30,000 licences issued
by the General Post Office, and it seemed an ideal topic to base a
revue upon. Yet *Listening In*, believed by its originators to be
devastatingly topical, was staged at the expensive and centrally
situated Apollo Theatre to founder after twenty-six performances.
It took a long time for managers to realise that intimate revue had
to have a star to carry it, and that certain theatres were more suitable to the form than others, just as Daly's and the Gaiety, equally
devoted to musical comedy, drew specific audiences. A Daly's
musical comedy could fail at the Gaiety, and vice versa.

In the same year that *Listening In* faltered, Beatrice Lillie was scoring a great hit at the Little Theatre with *Nine o'Clock Revue*. Jack Hulbert and Cicely Courtneidge left musical comedy, and established the Little Theatre as a home for revue, but later they moved to larger theatres, to the Apollo in 1925 with *By the Way* and to the Adelphi with *The House That Jack Built* in 1929. An expensive production of *Round in Fifty*, a re-hash of Jules Verne at the London Hippodrome, did extremely well; a much-applauded novelty was a film sequence of a race between an Atlantic liner and a motor launch. The writer of *Round in Fifty* was Sax Rohmer, alias Arthur Ward, a prolific author of thrillers featuring Dr Fu Manchu, and the star was George Robey.

Robey was one of the principal properties of Sir Oswald Stoll, and a furore broke out when it was announced that Robey was to star in a new revue to be staged at the Opera House, Covent Garden. The holy of holies was to be penetrated by a red-nosed comic. Reporters closed in on Robey's London flat to make certain that he was going to appear in what the press called a 'Jazzaganza' and Robey suggested that he was considering a first entrance as Lohengrin with the swan on a snaffle. With pre-production publicity on a par with this, *You'd Be Surprised* was a sell-out when it opened on 22 January 1923, despite its being an American production with the accent on dancing and no room in the confusion for Robey to sport himself.

You'd Be Surprised was an unintentioned return to Victorian extravaganza. Classical ballet had first been exposed on the music hall stage with the cry 'Culture for the masses' and in this Covent Garden revue masters and mistresses of Russian ballet such as Leonide Massine and Ninette de Valois were involved in a muddle that included Arabian acrobats, the popular Savoy Havana Band, and a parody of 'The green eye of the little yellow god' called 'The green fly on the little yellow dog'. The discomfited reasoned that spectacular revue was another name for a gaudy variety show, and when in 1924 *Leap Year* was produced, with Robey rendering Albert Chevalier's 'My old dutch', the tribute from one old trouper to another, suspicions seemed to be justified that it was music hall sliding back under another name. Nevertheless, *Leap Year* ran for 471 performances.

It seemed to many outsiders that revue was an undemanding genre, and professionals of the calibre of Edgar Wallace, that 40,000-words-a-week phenomenon, moved in. Unlike some, he was aware of the pitfalls:

> Some reverence is indeed due to the 'book' of a revue, for healthy as it may seem to the onlooker, it is foredoomed to extinction even before it has undergone the test of trial. No revue, at any rate no successful revue, bears any resemblance to the revue as it is at first suggested by the enthusiastic author . . . A revue is built up step by step and almost line by line as the rehearsals proceed . . . You put in a line, and take out a line there; you change one piece of 'business' for another; you alter the sequence of dances and scenes; you even bully the composer into revising his score and inserting a bar here and there to make your dances or your production numbers more effective.

Wallace haunted rehearsals, counting the laughs and making calculations of the number that might be expected on the opening night, and during actual performances he used a mechanical gadget to tabulate them. His revue *The Rainbow* ran for 113 performances in 1923, and Wallace turned his attention to the more profitable crime plays, such as *The Ringer*.

The best writers of revue had to be in tune with the spirit of the times, had to be participants rather than onlookers, ready to prick the balloon of pomposity and preferably able to compose, perform, and direct. The revue form might have been made for Noel Coward, born in 1899, who had performed in Barrie's *Peter Pan* as early as 1913. In 1923 he achieved great successes with his mordant play *The Vortex* and the revue *London Calling*, followed by *On with the Dance* (1925) and *This Year of Grace* (1928).

London Calling had Coward as co-author with Ronald Jeans of the book, as performer, and as composer and lyric writer. It included a satire on the Sitwell family, stigmatised as the Swiss Family Whittlebot which consisted of sister Hernia, dressed in undraped dyed sacking, Brother Gob, in cycling breeches, and Brother Sago. Osbert Sitwell was not amused, and later Coward declared, 'To this day I am still a little puzzled as to why that light-hearted burlesque should have aroused him, his brother, and his sister to such paroxysms of fury. But the fact remains that it did, and I believe still does.'

Coward was assisted by a talented band of performers, including Maisie Gay, and in *This Year of Grace* she had eleven changes of costume, with a minute and a half for each change. *London Calling* saw the start of the stage association between Coward and Gertrude Lawrence, a refugee from the heavily mystical pre-war *The Miracle* in which she was a child dancer. Coward was also able to utilise the talents of Ernest Thesiger and Douglas Byng, and in 1925, in *On with the Dance*, Alice Delysia singing 'Poor little rich girl'.

The wit and the humour, the cleverness at the expense of passing vogues, all these have lost their point. The wit is displayed better in the Noel Coward plays of the period such as *Hay Fever*, but the songs emerge from the wreckage of obsessive topicality. Only by chance were the songs for *On with the Dance* written by Coward, for the composer for this revue was Philip Braham. At the end Braham found that he had only three numbers marked up to him.

For *This Year of Grace* Coward wrote two songs that were as good as anything produced by the American masters of between-the-wars popular song—'A room with a view' and 'Dance, little lady', a song that encapsulated the spirit of the time, sung by Sonnie Hale, danced by Lauri Devine, with masks by Oliver Messel:

> Though you're only seventeen,
> Far too much of life you've seen,
> Syncopated child . . .
> But I know it's vain
> Trying to explain
> While there's this insane
> Music in your brain.

In this particular song Noel Coward showed himself a master of the new piquant harmonies codified by Cole Porter and

George Gershwin in America, and he also poked gentle fun at jazz mannerisms. In another song in the revue, 'Teach me to dance like Grandma', given to Jessie Matthews, he propounded ideas of the kind rapturously embraced by the fuddy-duddies:

> Black Bottoms, Charlestons!
> What wind blew them in?
> Monkeys do them in Zoos.

Jessie Matthews was an especially good find for revue. Born in 1907 in Soho, she was the quintessential flapper, long-legged, slim, with big saucer eyes. Starting her performing career as a chicken in an Irving Berlin number, she went to America as a chorus girl, having the good fortune to replace Gertrude Lawrence for a time. Her singing of two fine songs of the period, 'My heart stood still' and 'Dancing on the ceiling', marked her as a coming star.

One of the characteristics that contributed to her success was her versatility, not only as a dancer and a singer but in her ability to americanise. She became the perfect medium not only for the pert and romantic songs of the British composers, but also for the sophisticated urban songs of the Americans. She was the epitome of the age, as many of her colleagues in revue manifestly were not, and with her *gamine* look she became an object for emulation.

The songs from the revues that have lasted best were generally of an elegaic order, and quick-fire numbers, with a few notable exceptions, were forgotten when the shows ended. 'I'm crazy on the Charleston' and 'There's a trick in pickin' a chicken' (sung by Cicely Courtneidge in *Clowns in Clover* of 1927) made little permanent impact. They are as remote today as the spoken business, such as the skit on broadcasting talks 'Atmospherics' from *The Charlot Show of 1926*, or Ruth Draper doing 'The Secrets of Good Health' from *Clowns in Clover*, or 'Cleansing the stage' from *By the Way* (1925) which was, theatrical in-fighting indeed, a burlesque on *Spring Cleaning* by Frederick Lonsdale.

A good deal of American music was used in British revue, and paralleled the increasing americanisation of popular entertainment

Jessie Matthews created a new kind of look to feature in fashion magazines and on sheet music covers

in dance hall, theatre, and cinema. In 1921 the dance team of Dorothy Dickson and Carl Hyson was imported by Cochran for *London, Paris and New York* at the London Pavilion. *Rockets* of 1922 used a number that was almost incomprehensible to London ears, 'Klaxon horn jazz'. *The Music Box Revue* of 1923 was a straightforward American product with lyrics and music by Irving Berlin, and in the same year C. B. Cochran brought over Florence Mills to front the second half of his revue *Dover Street to Dixie*.

The novelty of Florence Mills was that she was black. She hoped that by her acting, singing, and dancing she would persuade the white world that Negroes were not just comic coons. She looked on herself as an ambassador, as Paul Robeson was to do in *Show Boat*. She brought with her a coloured orchestra, and the combination was too much for the government. The Minister of Labour, on the grounds that there was a great deal of unemployment, put pressure on managers, and black revues were withdrawn. The film *The Covered Wagon* was put on in place of Florence Mills and her company of plantation singers, though no one thought to ask how this substitution would help the unemployment situation. Nevertheless Florence Mills was to triumph in 1926 when Cochran brought *Blackbirds* to the Pavilion. Florence Mills had a big impact not only on theatregoers but on intellectuals, and Constant Lambert wrote a piano piece, 'Elegiac Blues', in memory of her when she died young. At the grave-side there was mass-singing of 'Bye-bye, blackbird'.

Despite the General Strike, 1926 saw spectacular revue going full tilt; a great success at the Palladium was *Palladium Pleasures*, which included Lorna and Toots Pounds singing one of the great 1920s hits, 'Valencia'. This revue reminded many of the audience of a return to pre-war standards, with less than usual of the ribald *double-entendre*, and value for money in twenty-two numbers. There were, it was calculated, two gross of legs in the beauty chorus, and three good comedians, including Billy Merson who appeared as an Australian cricketer, an umbrella merchant, a singing taxi-driver, and as Sir Gerald du Maurier in a parody of *The Last of Mrs. Cheyney*, a popular melodrama of the period.

'Valencia', one of the hits of 1926

There was some confusion about what the sketch 'Mothers of the World' set out to achieve, a series of lullabies that took place 'in a cathedral with New Art stained glass, the stone cubicles of the mothers of Ireland, Russia, Japan and Italy being guarded by men in full armour'. A 'March of the Crusaders', enacted by women, and a snake dance, were reckoned to be unimpressive, but Anton Dolin and Iris Rowe brought quality into their ballet. There were real cars on stage, and a nostalgic glance was cast at bygone days as the show ended with the old musical-comedy composer Leslie Stuart playing his own tunes at the piano. No doubt many of the members of the audience wondered whether the Vivian Ellis tunes of the main body of the show would match those that Stuart played—'Little dolly daydream', 'Lily of Laguna', and 'Soldiers of the Queen'.

In many ways the General Strike was a watershed. It demonstrated that life was real and earnest, and although Charlot, the Co-optimists, and Coward continued to espouse the cause of revue, the medium did not seem capable of any great development. There were new gimmicks. In *One Dam Thing After Another* (1927) one of the sensations was the girl jazz pianist Edythe Baker who performed 'The Birth of the Blues' by Ray Henderson. The music for most of this revue was written by Richard Rodgers, an American who was to establish a stranglehold on popular music. To many, revue was becoming tired, and the zip that had characterised the pioneer efforts was missing. It was ceasing to be metropolitan and becoming suburban, with lack-lustre sketches typified by 'The ever open door' in *The House That Jack Built* (1929) where 'Henry Carroway' (good for a laugh) settled 'the knick-knacks at the semi-detached villa in Harringay'.

Other revues were variety shows in disguise, with music hall artistes going through their routines as if in a dream. But a nightmare had been enfolded to management: the talkies, as promulgated by Al Jolson, the Singing Fool, had arrived. In 1928 Hannen Swaffer walked into the Duke of York's Theatre and announced: 'The theatre is dead. I have just seen it die.' He had been to the pictures.

The provincial theatre caught the blast first, but in London a

The Gaiety, prominent in Edwardian musical comedy, was in decline, and was even forced to stage music hall to keep solvent (Wonderful London)

new theatre actually opened, the Piccadilly. The only snag was that it was not in Piccadilly. The great musical-comedy houses of the Edwardians, Daly's and the Gaiety, were on the slippery slope, and only the London Pavilion with Noel Coward's *This Year of Grace* looked healthy. As if to comfort the despairing, three more theatres were opened in 1929, the Dominion, Tottenham Court Road, built on the site of Meux's Brewery and a fair distance away from theatreland proper, the tiny Duchess in Catherine Street, and one even more remote than the Dominion, the Streatham Hill Theatre, seating 2,700.

As if searching for the safe formula, Cochran put on *Wake Up and Dream* at the Streatham Hill Theatre, with music by Cole Porter and two excellent songs, 'What is this thing called love?' and 'Let's do it'. But the long agony of the musical theatre was to begin, and already speculators were busy converting theatres into picture houses. Musical comedy and revue had managed to survive the gramophone, the wireless, and the silent movie, but the talkie was too much to cope with, though non-stop revue was a palliative measure and after a time the discriminating realised that most of the talking pictures were abysmally low in intellectual content.

The music hall, it seemed, had already been dealt its death blow. By the end of the 1920s there were less than 100 music halls in the whole of Great Britain. The musical theatre could have found some consolation in the fact that the music hall experienced a resurgence in the 1930s, had management at that time known. Many of the musical comedy and revue stars went into films, including Jack Hulbert, Cicely Courtneidge, Jack Buchanan and Jessie Matthews, but many of them remained in West End theatre.

Against all the odds there were still enormous successes. The 1920s ended with the musical *Bitter Sweet* clocking up 673 performances, and a home-bred British musical *Mr. Cinders* doing well after a slow start. Its chief song was 'Spread a little happiness'. The uplift song was back, and it was desperately needed.

CHAPTER TWO

MUSICAL COMEDY AND OPERETTA

THE WAR CUT off the supply of European musical comedies and operettas, but no one seemed to mind when there were offerings such as *Maid of the Mountains* and *Chu Chin Chow*. *Chu Chin Chow* ran for the period 1916–21, earned its author Oscar Asche £200,000, and revived an interest in the exotic. In 1922 the Drury Lane Theatre management spent £40,000 on the staging of *Decameron Nights*, which had lavish sets depicting the Hanging Gardens of Babylon and St Mark's in Venice.

Putting on opulent musicals had always been an expensive pastime, and during the war the rentals of West End theatres had increased enormously; some managements paying £80 a week rent before the war found that the figure now being asked ranged from £300 to £400 a week. By 1926 the average play cost £1,300 a week, and Sir Alfred Butt stated that it was impossible to put a musical comedy on for less than £2,000 a week. A stall seat cost approximately the same as before the war, but the cheaper seats had gone up; a pit seat that had cost 2s 6d in 1914 was 4s ten years later.

Initially the increased basic costs in staging musical shows were disregarded, for there was a post-war boom with plenty of money about and promise in further musicals by home-bred composers such as Harold Fraser Simpson who had written *Maid of the Mountains*, and in the quick-moving shows from America. Some

of the older musical-comedy composers were trying desperately
to be up to date. Ivan Caryll used ragtime in *The Little Café* and
the fox-trot in the 1919 *The Girl behind the Gun* (also called
Kissing Time).

Unfortunately for Simpson, one swallow does not make a
summer, and none of his later musical comedies created much of
a stir, but *The Girl behind the Gun* at the new Winter Garden
Theatre, on the site of the Old Mogul music hall, did well with
George Grossmith and Leslie Henson, Yvonne Arnaud and
Phyllis Dare. Other offerings to a war-weary audience were not so
successful. The Empire, no longer a variety theatre, came a
cropper on a semi-educational musical with an Indian setting,
Sunshine of the World, and Montagu Phillips's *The Rebel Maid* at
the same theatre fell between two stools and was described as
heavy light opera.

With the ending of *Chu Chin Chow* it was expected that Oscar
Asche's follow-up, *Cairo*, would continue where his 2,288-
performances winner left off, but it was not to be, and this
'mosaic in music and mime' with music by Percy Fletcher
(1879–1932), not by *Chu Chin Chow*'s Frederic Norton, lingered
on for a respectable but disappointing 267 performances. Once
again, formula writing had failed, and only the American imports
showed any sign of being acceptable to the wider public. The new
school was represented by Jerome Kern's *Sally*, which included
the popular 'Look for the silver lining'. Kern followed this up
with *The Cabaret Girl*, which had the lively number 'Dancing
time', and *The Beauty Prize* which, like contemporary revues,
used a topical theme in 'You can't make love by wireless'. The
book by P. G. Wodehouse ensured that there was some style in
the words as well as in the music.

These post-war American musical comedies put the genre
firmly on the map, and made Kern, then in his mid-thirties, a
household name. He had been in the musical-comedy business
ten years, and had established his credentials as one of the coming
men in 1914 when he contributed one of the best of all popular
songs, 'They didn't believe me', to an otherwise undistinguished
musical *The Girl from Utah*, most of the music for which was

Kissing Time

M.H.Lawrence.

IVAN CARYLL
CHAPPELL

Kissing Time *by Ivan Caryll was typical of the kind of home-bred product that was presently to be swamped by the American musical*

*The Girl from Utah
contributed one of the
best of all popular songs,
'They didn't believe me'*

written by Sidney Jones and Paul Rubens. It was a common practice to leave to new writers the first few tunes in a show, for the customary late arrivals made certain that the audience did not settle down until well into the first act, and it did not seem economical to waste expensively commissioned music on it.

The failure of *Cairo* and the indifferent response to other post-war musicals made American contributions a welcome feature of the West End stage, but it was too early to determine whether the public was merely reacting to the novel. In Edwardian times, when matters were uncertain the remedy had been to put on Viennese operetta, but Emerich Kalman's *The Gipsy Princess* (1921) was not another *Merry Widow*, nor was Oscar Straus's *The Last Waltz*, though the latter had the distinction of being the first musical play to be broadcast from a theatre—the Gaiety was conveniently next door to wireless station 2LO, Marconi House.

Musicals of the time were labelled musical comedies, musical plays, comic opera, plays with music, or light opera, without anyone bothering about definitions. If there was a distinction it was that the Europeans preferred the term operetta, and in theory the music was more integrated with the action than in the musical comedy, where there was no reluctance to throw in a show-stopper without reference to the action. The term operetta had more class.

Like *The Gipsy Princess* and *The Last Waltz*, *Lilac Time*, a cobbled-together pot-boiler with music by Schubert, was unquestionably an operetta. Although it had been turned down by one management it proved to be a considerable triumph, and this seemed to indicate that there was still a lot of mileage in Viennese *kitsch*. It seemed the right time to revive the Edwardian phenomenon, and back came *The Merry Widow* at Daly's.

The crystal ball had misted up, for the revival failed, but undaunted its composer launched out into *The Three Graces*, and only when this and its successor *Frasquita* failed did it dawn on Lehar and management alike that *The Merry Widow* was a fluke. Not that *Frasquita* was any more ridiculous than dozens of other mid-European offerings, with its plot centring round a gipsy girl and mistaken identity, and it had José Collins in the lead.

The year of *Frasquita* (1925) was the year the American big battalions arrived on the scene with the operetta-type *Rose Marie*, music by Rudolf Friml, and the quintessence of all fast-moving musical comedies, considered by Arnold Bennett to be the best of them all, *No, No, Nanette*. This had music by Vincent Youmans, until then known in England by one popular song, 'Oh me, oh my, oh you', composed in 1921. Although not so well-known as Cole Porter or Gershwin, Youmans was one of the very greatest of the American composers of evergreens, obtaining the maximum effect from the repetition of three or four notes as in 'Tea for two' or 'Without a song'. He was considerably younger than Kern, and it was as a wartime sailor in the US Navy that he composed 'Hallelujah', showed it to the bandmaster, and had it

Rose Marie at the Drury Lane Theatre was one of the first American musicals to make the English product seem old-fashioned and threadbare (Wonderful London)

played ten years before it appeared in *Hit the Deck*. He contracted tuberculosis in 1934, from which he died in 1946, when he was only forty-seven.

The book of *No, No, Nanette* was not scrambled together anyhow but was based on a novel by May Edgington, produced as a play in 1920. The plot revolves round a hero who has a wife over-scrupulous in money matters, forcing him to spend his extra money upon lady friends at Nice, Bath, and Harrogate, and to lead a tortuously complicated existence. Innovations in *No, No, Nanette* included casting two middle-aged comedians, Joseph Coyne and George Grossmith, as the lovers, using a contemporary idiom with sets resolutely laid in flapper-land, and pace that made most of its fellow-musicals—including the stand-up-and-sing *Rose Marie*—seem ridiculously old-fashioned. Not surprisingly the hit song from the production, 'Tea for two', was the most recorded number of the 1925–6 season. In point of fact, *Rose*

Marie ran for longer than its rival, relying on spectacle rather than zip. It included a murder scene and a chorus of 100, a clutch of non-jazz tunes that were unadaptable and were therefore left alone by novelty and dance bands. It was succeeded by *The Desert Song*, beautifully timed to drop into the fashion for sheikhs.

The West End theatre was clearly dominated by American shows, with Kern and Youmans ready to consolidate their positions. There were two main strands—the contemporary real-life musicals with girls in bare legs such as *No, No, Nanette* and the flashy exotica, which were showing a tendency to become pretentious. This was especially in evidence with Sigmund Romberg, who was taken severely to task by the arbiter of London theatre, James Agate. Of Romberg's *Student Prince* he admitted that the melodies were fairly good in outline, but were 'so thinly orchestrated that the score must look like a skeleton'. As for the humour, it was more 'aggravation than relief'. He was allusive about *New Moon*, music by Romberg, book by Oscar Hammerstein II, bringing into the English language a new verb, 'to balfe' (derived from the Victorian composer, Balfe). 'To balfe, then, means to confound values generally, in the theatrical sense to elevate something to a position which it is not entitled to hold.'

But no one could say that the more skittish musical comedies were getting above themselves, though in 1927 Agate had a few words to say about George Gershwin's *Oh, Kay* which, he claimed, had no single spark of wit or even humour in it, while the music was 'largely made up of two tunes, one of which was plugged at least fourteen times'. Of another American musical, *Lido Lady*, words by Ronald Jeans, drifting over from the world of revue, and music by Richard Rodgers, he commented, 'Happy is the country which has no history and happier still is that musical comedy about which one can find nothing to say.'

Being American was not necessarily a guarantee of success, and in the year that saw *The Desert Song* succeed *Rose Marie*, Richard Rodgers's *Peggy Anne* was being given the thumbs down, and, although it did somewhat better, his *Lady Luck* did not shine so brilliantly as had been hoped by its backers. The

A scene from No, No, Nanette *(1925), perhaps the best of all
musical comedies* (Wonderful London)

Rose Marie type musical was inching towards opera, and Friml's
The Vagabond King fell between genres. Setting it in underworld
Paris in the days of Villon and with a chorus of thieves, at least
Friml found a new locale, and his score persuaded a middlebrow
audience that they were listening to high-class music. There was
an ambiguity about the form of the work, but none about the
mellifluous and over-sweet songs, the plums to be wrenched
from their setting. 'Only a rose' and 'The vagabonds' chorus'
could have fitted into any Edwardian musical, and picaresque
criminals together with the Red Indians from *Rose Marie* and
the sheikhs from *The Desert Song* could happily have languished
in the wings at performances of *The Merry Widow*, waiting for
their entrances and their big numbers.

Notwithstanding the uncertainty of the times, new theatres
were being opened in London—the Carlton and the Fortune in
1927, the Piccadilly in 1928—though the theatres most noted in
Edwardian times for their musicals, Daly's and the Gaiety, were
in eclipse, and anything staged there seemed to have the mark of

doom on it. The Gaiety even turned to two seasons of music hall after the musical *Topsy and Eva* flopped.

For theatregoers who were finding Romberg and company too cloying there was relief when Vincent Youmans's *Hit the Deck* opened at the Hippodrome. Ludicrous in plot but preserving the pace of *No, No, Nanette*, *Hit the Deck* was cleverly anglicised, with a sailor/reluctant lover sought out by Looloo, chased to China where bandits were being troublesome and providing a varied scene, and finally being brought to book against a highly idealised background of Plymouth quayside cottages. The part of the sailor was played by Stanley Holloway who brought to the role consistency and insight into character not usually found in musical comedy, and there was comic relief by the coloured servant Magnolia who, oddly enough, had the big number, 'Hallelujah', which cashed in on the fashion for Negro spirituals and imitation Negro spirituals. The theatre critic of *Punch*, always ready to knock down the counterfeit and the presumptuous, voted it 'a lively likeable show, mounted with a lavish realism that has no art nonsense about it'.

But even *Hit the Deck* was eclipsed by Kern's 1928 smash-hit *Show Boat*. *Show Boat* started off as a novel by Edna Ferber, said to have sold 320,000 copies. Cast with Marie Burke and Paul Robeson, the musical was able to cash in on the appeal of blues and a jazz feeling without bursting the bounds of realism. It provided perhaps more evergreen songs than any other musical of the period—'Ol' man river', 'Can't help lovin' dat man', 'Why do I love you?' and 'Make believe'. It was conceived on a large scale, with a time-span from the 1880s to the 1920s, yet had 'no art nonsense about it'. It demanded a cast of 144 and 14 scenes, and was lavish without being tricksy or gaudy.

The British musical comedy was not in the same league, and it was something of a surprise when *Bitter Sweet* made its appearance at His Majesty's Theatre, written, composed, and produced by Noel Coward. Coward was very much an in-figure of the period, but it was not supposed that his musical would make more than a temporary impact on the London scene with Kern, Cole Porter, Gershwin, and Youmans at their peak, ready to overwhelm London with further proof, if it was necessary, that they held the trump cards. *Bitter Sweet* also used a long time-span, from 1895 to the present, and Coward was craftsman enough to make the transition between costume and contemporary musical work. There was a note of astringency present that was rare amongst British musical-comedy composers uncertain of their target and bogged down with rhyming moon with June (though Coward did his share of that). In comparison with the American musicals, *Bitter Sweet* was old-fashioned, but it had style. The tunes have not worn as well as those by the Americans, or those in his own revues. 'I'll see you again', 'Tokay', and 'If love were all' do not come up to the standard, in either words or music, of 'A room with a view' or 'Dance, little lady'. The waltz 'I'll see you again' is Lehar's *Merry Widow* waltz song viewed through frosted glass.

Its success abashed the critics, and to confirm that the British musical was not going to lie down and die another long runner popped up at the Adelphi, though it had to be backed by Australian money. *Mr. Cinders* by Vivian Ellis was no world beater, but no one could say of it that it was run-of-the-mill, the kind of musical dismissed by Arnold Bennett when he visited the Gaiety in 1926:

> A rotten musical play, with a terrible chorus, and not enough music . . . It all seemed to me to be a bit sad. Generations of actors and actresses (in that same theatre, or in one on the same site) always talking and singing of love and fornication, and kisses and drink, and always in a piffling childish way . . .

Success was measured in the West End of London, though even steady money-makers had to recoup their initial outlay in provincial tours or in America. A few full houses did not make backers rich. But outside the sacred square mile of theatreland was the Lyric, Hammersmith, which had the temerity to run a 3½-year revival of the eighteenth-century *Beggar's Opera*, and also put on John Gay's other 'opera', *Polly*. The *Beggar's Opera*, wrote Arnold Bennett in his diary, was an affair of prodigious enthusiasm, and well done in some ways. Here is an absolutely English thing, understood by English artists and done by them excellently well so far as the limitations of their gifts would allow. The music is lovely, heavenly sometimes, and the dialogue always brilliant. Also it is daring and bawdy, with robust ideas about life. This is in my opinion one of the most wonderful entertainments I have ever seen.

Whether he was trying out ideas for a publicity leaflet is not known, but Arnold Bennett had shares in the Lyric, Hammersmith. The Lyric later put on *Tantivy Towers*, words by A. P. Herbert, music by Thomas Dunhill, and A. P. Herbert's Cockney opera *Derby Day*, which was greeted with raised eyebrows when it was transferred to the West End.

These ventures outside the magic West End proved that musicals with a minority appeal could survive in the hard-boiled world of 1920s commercialism. But survival was different from putting money into backers' pockets, and with small theatres out of the circuit and therefore obliged to charge low admission prices the moneyed looked, thought, and turned away. There was

The interior of Drury Lane Theatre, lavish and spectacular like its productions (Wonderful London)

no percentage in supporting the fringe theatre. Supply and demand dominated the musical comedy scene of the 1920s, and over all loomed the American influence, as a provider of shows and as the recipient of them (if suitably fashioned for the Broadway audience).

Small theatres, like small music halls, were at a disadvantage during the decade, though some of them, like the Lyric, Hammersmith, kept going. The money-spinners were concentrated in a handful of large theatres, with the Hippodrome, the Winter Garden Theatre, and the Drury Lane Theatre replacing the Gaiety and Daly's. We can see now the path musicals were following, increasingly American-orientated and culminating in *Oklahoma* and *West Side Story*, but at the time a fluke British hit and an unexpected American flop obfuscated the pattern. There were always arbitrary factors muddling the objective appraisal.

It is instructive to examine the whole of the London musical scene during the course of one year (1927–8):

Carlton, Haymarket	*The Yellow Mask*	Musical comedy by Edgar Wallace, music by Vernon Duke
	Good News	American musical comedy
Court, Sloane Square	*Cosi fan Tutte*	Light opera by Mozart
	The Secret Marriage	Comic opera by Cimarosa
Daly's, Cranbourne St	*Lilac Time*	Musical comedy with music by Franz Schubert
	Lady Mary	Musical comedy by Frederick Lonsdale, music by Albert Sirmay
Drury Lane, Catherine St	*Show Boat*	Musical comedy by Oscar Hammerstein II, music by Jerome Kern

Gaiety, Strand	*The Girl from Cook's*	Musical comedy by R.H. Burnside and Greatrex Newman, music by Raymond Hubbell and Jean Gilbert
	Marjolaine	Musical comedy by Louis N. Parker, music by Hugo Felix
	Topsy and Eva	Musical play by Catherine Cushing, music by the Duncan sisters
Hippodrome, Cranbourne St	*Hit the Deck*	Musical comedy by Hubert Osborne, music by Vincent Youmans
	That's a Good Girl	Musical comedy by Douglas Furber, music by Philip Charig and Joseph Meyer
His Majesty's, Haymarket	*Song of the Sea*	Musical play by Arthur Wimperis and Lauri Wylie, music by Eduard Kunneke
Lyceum, Wellington St	*Lumber Love*	Musical comedy by Leslie Stiles, music by Berte and Emmett Adams
Lyric, Hammersmith	*The Beggar's Opera*	By John Gay (revival)

	Love in a Village	By M. Bicker-staffe, with music arranged from Arne
Palace, Cambridge Circus	*Virginia*	Musical comedy by Herbert Clayton, Douglas Furber, R.P. Weston, and Bert Lee, music by Jack Waller and J.A. Tunbridge
Piccadilly, Denman St	*Blue Eyes*	Musical comedy by Guy Bolton and Graham John, music by Jerome Kern
Vaudeville, Strand	*Sylvia*	Comedy with music adapted from play by St. John Ervine
Winter Garden, Drury Lane	*So This Is Love*	Musical comedy by Stanley Lupino and Arthur Rigby, music by Hal Brody

Many of the composers and lyric writers concerned in these performances are lost in the footnotes of theatrical history. It would be interesting to know what happened to the Gaiety composing team, the Duncan sisters. It is a reflection on the night life of London that even with the competition of the cinema there were forty-three theatres in central London.

In a sense there is an omission in the entry for the Piccadilly, Denman St: *The Jazz Singer* Sound film with Vitaphone Synchronisation.

That gave cause for alarm all round. In 1929 the full-scale musical film was possible, resulting in Warner Brothers' *Gold Diggers of Broadway* and *Broadway Melody*.

CHAPTER THREE

RAGTIME INTO JAZZ

SHORTLY BEFORE WORLD WAR I ragtime had established itself in Britain in the form of new, pungent popular songs such as 'Alexander's ragtime band' and 'Hitchy-koo', used as the basis for novel dances and given wide coverage on gramophone records and in revue. *Hullo, Ragtime!* clocked up 451 performances at the London Hippodrome in 1912, and during the war sophisticated and lively revue was a welcome counterpoise to musical comedy. Revues with ragtime elements did extremely well; *Zig-zag* ran for 648 performances in 1917, and *Cheep* for 483.

Ragtime was ripe for development and exploitation, and jazz made its appearance, confusedly believed to be another aspect of ragtime, and even a novelty dance. The *Dancing Times* declared that 'five instruments form the foundation of a true "Jazz Band", namely the clarinet (playing violin parts), the cornet, the trombone, a "snappy" drummer, and a ragtime piano-player'. The musical director of the Coliseum thought that jazz was 'a piece of music entirely surrounded by noise'. The dancing teacher Egerton Welch compounded confusion by announcing that she was exhibiting and teaching three of America's latest dance crazes—the ramble, the three-step, and 'the Jazz'. Schools opened to teach the 'jazz-roll', the 'jazz-step' and the 'shimmy-jazz'.

The most important dancing instructress of the time, Mrs Vernon Castle, hastened to clear up misunderstanding. She said in November 1918:

On one point I am definite, there is no such dance as the 'Jazz', and anyone who tells you there is is wrong . . . the nigger bands at home 'Jazz' a tune, that is to say, they slur the notes, they syncopate, and each instrument puts in a lot of little fancy bits of its own . . . I have not come across a 'Jazz' Band in England, and I doubt if there is one.

There *were* bands that called themselves jazz bands, such as the Murray Club Jazz Band, but they were mainly novelty bands, though this was true to some degree of the first genuine jazz band to visit Britain from America, the Original Dixieland Jazz Band.

The band's first engagement was at the London Hippodrome in the George Robey revue *Joy Bells*. Robey hated what he called 'jungle music' and for him the ODJB, as the band has been known ever since, represented the degeneration of modern man. As the chief attraction of the show, Robey had powers that verged on the dictatorial, and the ODJB lasted for one night, being reduced to club work until it obtained a three-month season at the brand-new Hammersmith Palais de Danse, together with another American group, Billy Arnold's Novelty Jazz Band.

History has had few good words to say of the ODJB. Although jazz-inspired, it went to the Palais ready to play what the audience wanted. As the jazz critic Rex Harris wrote: 'What musical purity the O.D.J.B. possessed was lost in a wild helter-skelter of trombones played with the feet, funny hats, and saucepan-lid drum-kits.' The comedy jazz band suggested loose living, debauchery, and the worst excesses of the flesh.

Other American bands came to England, such as Art Hickman's New York-London Five, playing at the Criterion Roof, the Louisiana Jazz Band, the Paramount Six, Billy Madden's Crescent City Orchestra (the crescent city was New Orleans) and the first all-black group, the Jazz Kings. None of these played jazz, nor did Murray Pilcer and his Jazz Band, who advertised themselves in the following terms in the *Sound Wave* in March 1919:

The leader of the great Jazz Combination, who exercise their stupendous powers in disseminating torrential tones to thrill multitudes in the Metropolis, was invited to enlarge his popularity by placing a few samples on Winner [a record company]. He agreed, declaring he would make records that would eclipse Creation. Having put his cannonading party in effective positions, he divested himself of all clothing decency would permit, and fitted his feet, legs, arms and head to mediums for extracting sounds from many and varied instruments . . .

This megalomaniacal band made just two records. The numbers played were 'The wild wild women', 'K-K-K-Katy', 'I'm all bound round with the Mason Dixon Line', and 'That moaning trombone'. The sales talk and the bombast were typical of English jazz of the 1920s: sound and fury signifying nothing. The line-up of this band could be duplicated a hundred times in dance hall and recording studio, hotel and cabaret: trumpet, trombone, alto saxophone doubling clarinet, tenor saxophone, violin, piano, banjo, double bass, and drums.

Because professional musicians, conscious that they were on to a good thing, made such a noise about jazz there was a tendency to take them seriously. If they called themselves jazz bands, it was thought, then they must be jazz bands, and when dance-band musicians pontificated solemnly on their Call they were listened to with awe. One of the doyens of English jazz of the 1920s was Jack Hylton who in 1926 was leading the Kit Kat Club band. He told the *Melody Maker*, 'like a debutante, jazz has developed during ten years from its blatant beginning, and its crude gaucheries into a thing of charm and grace, wherein the skill of musician, composer, and arranger is exercised to the utmost'. The American jazz musicians would not have understood what he was talking about. Grace, charm, arrangers, what had they to do with jazz? Hylton continued:

The public wants it and will not let it go. Surely that is the great and only test. Music, like newspapers, books, carpet slippers, top hats, dormice [*dormice?*] and other things, is at the mercy of the law of supply and demand, and if there is no demand, then syncopation dies away unmourned.

A cover for a now-forgotten revue depicting everyman's idea of sophistication, jazz band and all

Jack Hylton perpetuated the confusion about the nature of jazz. To him, and most others, syncopation *was* jazz. To Dr Henry Coward, responsible for a resurgence of the choral tradition in the north of England, a syncopated band was a synonym for a jazz band:

> A syncopated orchestra is good at killing time
> Or turning into balderdash a symphony sublime.

There were assumptions about the nature of jazz, but few thought hard about it and made sensible definitions. What was the difference between ragtime and jazz? Jelly Roll Morton made his contribution: 'Ragtime is a certain type of syncopation and only certain tunes can be applied in that idea. But jazz is a style that can be applied to any type of tune.' Peter Gammond and Peter Clayton described jazz as a racy, slang-ridden musical language, a conversational music and a dialect, tending to be neurotic and restless. The raciness is achieved by regular rhythm, the language through syncopated distortion of the common musical language. It was not intended as an ill-bred attempt to knock the stuffing or take the mickey out of traditional music, though it was often thought that the height of the jazzman's ambition was to jazz the classics until the pips squeaked, that innocuous sport still with us.

Very few people of the 1920s realised that the essence of jazz was improvisation, or that the metronomic beat of a dance band was not the same as the driving rhythm of the jazz drummer. These arcane secrets were kept hidden from most of the band leaders, shackled by convention to arrangements and the demands of dancers. A few learned differently when they were daring enough to import genuine jazz musicians such as the banjoist Pete Mandell, who joined the Savoy Orpheans in 1923, though there is little evidence to suggest that the leader of the Orpheans, Debroy Somers, incorporated dangerous ideas into his programmes. Perhaps there were some doubts sown about the nature of jazz when the very able jazz pianist of the Original Dixieland Jazz Band was playing off-duty.

Jazz was a rallying cry for the forces of reaction. In his book *Music Ho!* (1934) Constant Lambert wrote about 'the crusty old colonels, the choleric judges and beer-sodden columnists who imagine they represent the European tradition, murmuring "swamp stuff", "jungle rhythms", "negro decadence" whenever they hear the innocent and anodyne strains of the average English jazz band'. Innocence, indeed, marked the English jazz musician as a creature far removed from his American counterpart. The Roaring Twenties of legend were muted into a sound, half-growl, half-purr. What had Jack Hylton, Debroy Somers, Jack Payne, or Corelli Windeatt (conductor of the London Dance Orchestra, a prolific recorder of ragtime and quasi-jazz) in common with Louis Armstrong, Cow Cow Davenport, Sidney Bechet, or Joe Oliver?

There were journalists in plenty to report on manifestations of the *zeitgeist*; they had applied the label 'The Jazz Age' and were stuck with it. The Viscountess Molesworth was cornered by the *Daily Mail* regarding her love of jazz. Watching a dance she 'fell to meditating on the mystery of jazz . . . the music was quiet, haunting, subdued — and syncopated . . . I tried to penetrate the secret of syncopation . . .' Philosophising, she went on to say:

> On the whole there seemed to be something rather wonderful about the New Music. Syncopation may not be high art; the jazz band may be crude, unaesthetic, and lacking in true beauty. But, looking into the future, I seemed to see the possibility of a new kind of music—real music—arising out of the modern craze for syncopated strains.

Nobody, unfortunately, asked the viscountess what exactly she was listening to. From her description one would have thought it was J. H. Squire's Celeste Octet, anti-jazz and genteel, but jazz was wrapped up not only with syncopation (a new word for the non-musical) but with the tone colour of the bands due to the introduction of saxophones. The saxophone had been invented in 1846, and had long been used in military bands. Bizet and Massenet employed the saxophone in works of unblemished respectability, but its modern vogue started during the war when 'novelty solos'

*British jazz musicians thought themselves the genuine
article. With few exceptions they were not*

were played on tenor saxophones during the intermissions of
West End theatres.

The 1926 band of Jack Hylton consisted of three saxophones,
three brass, and four rhythm instruments. W. W. Seabrook stated
in 1924 that 'Every legitimate night club proprietor knows that
he might as well be out of business as to be without a saxophone
performer.'

A distinctive tone colour was also given to jazz bands by the
muted trumpet, which was thought by those not acquainted with
symphonic music to be a purely jazz device. About 1924 a dozen
'wow-wow' mutes were sent over from New York, and were
sold within two hours. Mutes came in a variety of shapes and
sizes with exotic names including the 'Pierrot', 'Sambo', 'Peke

Dog', 'Long Clothes Baby', 'Toy Soldier', and 'Blush Rose'.

Many of the diehards refused to believe that jazz was happening. In a court case Mr Justice Eve asked in bewilderment 'What is a sax?' and when told that it was an instrument resembling a cornet to be found in jazz bands, he asked whether it was wind or strings. There was a mystique about the saxophone, only partially exploded when the comedian Lupino Lane learned how to play it in a month and impersonated Jack Hylton, Paul Whiteman and Ted Lewis on the stage. The widespread use of the saxophone had an important effect technically in that it down-graded the banjo and made the sound of 1920s popular music distinctly different from the piano and banjo orientated ragtime of the previous decade. (Ragtime was originally conceived solely for piano, which in turn was used because it could do all that four banjos could accomplish.)

Jazz musicians were widely envied by the young men of the time, and many of them tried to emulate their heroes by learning the slang or one of the favoured instruments. An advertisement in one of the musical journals reveals the extent of the secret language of the cognoscenti:

AT LIBERTY, TROMBONIST.—Hot and sweet, Plenty pep. Read and fake, can sing. Play in tune, gold outfit, tuxedo, double at drums, dirt and flash, hot sock cymbal. Ham lay off. Young and good looking. Some violin when needed, double-stop and goofus.

The *Musical Times* confessed itself beaten, though it is a code that is open to cracking. Hot, sweet, and pep are self-explanatory, and fake would be pretending to read music but playing by ear. It is customary for present-day buskers to put music on their stands at good-quality dances (as the author was a dance-band musician for several years he knows about some of these tricks). The claim that the advertiser plays in tune indicates that he considered most trombonists played out of tune, and shows him up as a tyro. Gold outfit and tuxedo (the fashionable dinner jacket of the time) are to do with dress; doubling is playing another instrument. Dirt was jazz feeling, flash was swank, swing, hot sock cymbal probably means that he enjoys banging away at the hi-hat, the name given to two cymbals set horizontally and clashed together by means of a foot pedal. Ham lay off is too arcane for us today, and goofus is funny business, playing trombone with the feet and related antics.

One of the easiest of instruments for amateurs was the banjo, and there were as many advertisements offering to teach the banjo as there were by schools of journalism offering to teach authorship. Typical was the advertisement published by the Paganini School of Music, Hawick: 'Boys, learn the Banjo, and be prepared for the next boom in Jazz', though by the 1920s the banjo had been overtaken as an amateur's instrument by the ukelele or ukelele-banjo.

The ukelele was the true name of the Hawaiian guitar, a smaller instrument than the true guitar; it is played legato and emits a wailing sound. It became very popular in the 1930s when there was a vogue for mock-Hawaiian bands. The ukelele-banjo was much more common in the 1920s than the ukelele; it was a

Jazz bands meant funny hats, tricks, and horse-play (Pageant of the Century)

version of the banjo with a shorter neck, and was used to strum
an accompaniment to popular songs. It was made famous by
George Formby, and in sheet music of the 1920s there is a
diagrammatic ukelele part set above the voice line, with details
of how to finger the relevant chord.

An instrument that found its way into the public domain was
the mouth organ, sometimes called the harmonica. This was
used on novelty records, but because bands were not amplified
the mouth organ, with its thin sound, was not often used out
of the studio. By 1928, 50 million mouth organs were being
exported from Germany a year (22 million to the United States)
and the industry supported 22,000 workers.

The bands that played the pale simulacrum of jazz were not
necessarily jazz bands. Jazz, misunderstood but played because
that was what the public wanted, was a *lingua franca* of the 1920s,
and among the bands that entered into competition with Jack
Hylton and his colleagues was the band of Kneller Hall, the head-
quarters of army music. After a trombone quartet performing
music from *Tannhäuser* and twelve saxophones in a saxophone
concerto, the military band played, reported the *Melody Maker*, a
'red hot jazz number' with 'breaks, modern American effects',
though the band was short on 'gliss' (=glissando, using the
slide of a trombone to run up and down the scale and very
popular amongst the funny-hat men and cinema orchestra
musicians).

Other respectable bands that should have known better than
intrude into this world were the Band of the Honourable Artillery
Company, the City Police Band of Birmingham (with 'Tiger's
Tail March'), the Band of the Coldstream Guards (with 'Hello,
Hawaii, how are you?' and 'The Tickle Toe'), and the Band of
the Scots Guards (with 'Everything is peaches down in Georgia').

The repertoires of the jazz bands were predominantly composed
of American music, and varied depending on the location. The
bands were forced to adapt their libraries for the succession of
dance crazes that swept through the 1920s, the most famous of
which was the Charleston, danced by Negroes in 1923, demonstrated by Annette Mills and Robert Sielle at the Hotel Metropole,

The Piccadilly Hotel was regarded as a plum fixture by the dance bands of the time (Wonderful London)

London, in 1925, reaching its apotheosis at the Charleston Ball held at the Albert Hall in December 1926.

The Charleston was preceded by the Blues, transmogrified in Britain into the fox-trot, and was followed by the Black Bottom which came into fashion in 1927 just as the Charleston was dying out. The Black Bottom did not enjoy the astonishing success of the Charleston as it had to compete with other dances such as the Lindy Hop and the Bam Bam Bamy, not to mention the dance that was to eclipse all others, the quickstep.

Unquestionably the jazz bands of the period were at their most successful in the dance hall, and most of them were resident bands of hotels where their prime role was to supply music to dance to. Birt Firman's band was at the Carlton Hotel, Teddie Brown, virtuoso of the xylophone, was leader of the Café de Paris band, Sidney Bliss was at the Metropolitan, and Hugo Rignold— today a renowned conductor of serious music—was leader of the band at Kettner's. In essence, the so-called jazz bands were really dance bands feeling their way towards the swing bands of the 1930s; they had been persuaded by their own publicity that they were something other.

The comments by American bandleaders were treated as sour grapes. The American Alex Hyde, doing a season at the Piccadilly Hotel, said: 'You may say for me that any "ching joint" band in New York, Chicago or Philadelphia, if it were transported to England . . . would make any English band look sick.' But even in America there was a wide gap between fashionable white musicians and the earthy Negro jazzmen.

The speculation that jazz bands were dance bands flying the wrong flag is borne out by the tunes they played: 'Silver Lining', 'The greatest lad we ever had', 'Horsey, keep your tail up', 'Hawaiian eyes', 'Let's go to Wembley', 'If we could live on love', 'Honeymoon chimes', 'It gets you hot and bothered', 'Down-hearted blues', 'I found a four leaf clover', 'Yes, we have no bananas' (a Debroy Somers speciality), 'Pasadena' (the hit of 1924, with sheet music sales of a million), and the roll call of American hits—'Ain't she sweet?' by Milton Ager (1927), 'Baby face' by Harry Akst (1926), and 'Yes, sir, that's my baby' by Walter Donaldson (1925). If the bands really wanted to feel that they were playing 100 per cent jazz they could revert to the classics of the Original Dixieland Jazz Band, 'Tiger rag', 'Sensation rag' and 'Livery stable blues'.

The New Music, as Viscountess Molesworth described it, played havoc with the old-time ballads. In 1928 the *Musical Standard* stated:

> Jazz with its brisk and grotesque rhythms has ousted our dismal ballads if it has done nothing else, and the waltz, declining into a state of Turkish delight, has revived under this influence. Savagery in art is a tonic—when art is too tepid it is in danger of petering out.

A large number of intellectuals thought that jazz had a part to play in the future of serious music, and Darius Milhaud went to the Hammersmith Palais to hear Billy Arnold's band. 'What a long way we have travelled', he declared enthusiastically, 'from the gypsies who before the war used to pour their insipid mawkish strains intimately into one's ear.' In 1919 the Swiss conductor Ernest Ansermet wrote about the young jazz clarinettist Sidney Bechet, who 'can say nothing of his art, save that he follows his "own way" and when one thinks that "his own way" is perhaps the highway the whole world will swing along tomorrow . . .' Carl Engel, Chief of the Music Division of the Library of Congress, wished to rid jazz of some of its unsavoury connotations:

> To a great many minds the word 'jazz' implies frivolous or obscene deportment. Let me ask what the word 'sarabande' suggests to you? I have no doubt that to most of you it will mean everything that is diametrically opposed to 'jazzing'. When you hear mention of a 'sarabande', you think of Bach's, of Handel's slow and stately airs . . . Yet the sarabande, when it was first danced in Spain, about 1588, was probably far more shocking to behold than is the most shocking jazz today [1922].

Stravinsky was sent a parcel of published jazz (somewhat of a contradiction in terms), and he found it 'enchanting me by its

WONDERFUL ONE

(Waltz Song)

Words by
DOROTHY TERRISS

Music by
**PAUL WHITEMAN,
FERDIE GROFÉ**
and
**MARSHALL
NEILAN**

As Played by
**PAUL
WHITEMAN'S
Famous
Orchestra**

2/- net

LONDON
FRANCIS, DAY & HUNTER
138-140, Charing Cross Road, W.C. 2

NEW YORK
LEO FEIST, INC.,
231-5, West 40th Street

Authorised for sale in the British Empire, exclusive
of Canada, Newfoundland and Australasia,
but not elsewhere

*It was clear that many of the so-called jazz bands were not playing
jazz at all, and Paul Whiteman's 'Wonderful One' was just an
ordinary commercial tune*

truly popular appeal, its freshness, and the novel rhythm which so distinctly revealed its Negro origin'. Jazz mannerisms and devices found their way into Stravinsky's own music, into Milhaud's *La Création du Monde*, into operas by Kurt Weill, into Ravel's Violin Sonata and into works by Constant Lambert. By no stretch of the imagination can any of these pieces be called popular.

Symphonic jazz was another matter. This was the attempt to rid jazz in one fell swoop of its funny hat and its Negro images, to make it respectable and persuade the middle-brows that it was not as bad as it had been painted. The most characteristic work of the synthesisers was George Gershwin's *Rhapsody in Blue*, described by Constant Lambert as 'the hybrid child of a hybrid'. Gershwin followed this with his Piano Concerto in F in 1925, and this succeeded in persuading waverers that jazz in the right hands (preferably white) could be tolerable. Many other attempts to take the charge out of jazz were made, especially by Paul Whiteman, the doyen of 'symphonic syncopation'.

Whiteman had served with the US Navy during World War I, and had been leader of a forty-piece band. On demobilisation he settled for an eight-piece group, but he was so successful at taming jazz that he built up a big band, which visited Britain in 1923 under the maestro. The band was made up of two trumpets, two trombones, two French horns, a flute, saxophones, clarinets and oboes, a string section of eight violins, two string basses, banjo, piano, and drums. With a line-up like this it would have been difficult to play jazz even if Whiteman had wanted to.

Confident that he was giving jazz an improved image, Whiteman used to start his programme with jazz as it was before the Second Coming. A rapturous listener recorded that 'there was all the blare and discord and the lack of melody as we used to know it, and, alas, as we still know it, in some places. Then he played the same tune as he would render it today, and in a moment one realised what Whiteman means when he talks of "symphonising syncopation" '.

Paul Whiteman's sleek, streamlined band was certainly not a Mickey Mouse outfit like some of the British but quite evidently a swing band. Swing was what the British public *really* liked, and one or two British musicians got the message. In 1926 Whiteman made a second visit to Britain, this time with a twenty-seven-piece orchestra, and did a long tour through the provinces. He was treated with less sympathy by the non-musical press which spoke of his shattering explosions, jingly tunes, and grotesque forms, and he was now in competition with other American bands. These included, almost for the first time, a genuine jazz group—Duke Ellington's, 'a coloured unit in which the expected faults of coon bands—a noticeable crudeness and somewhat poor tone—are by no means so apparent as usual'.

British audiences were at last getting the genuine article, although they did not know it. One of the best smaller groups of the time, Jelly Roll Morton and his Red Hot Peppers, was described as 'hopelessly old-fashioned in style, even if the musicians can play their instruments'. Good jazz bands even infiltrated the fastnesses of the Savoy Hotel, and in 1928 Fred Elizalde, a Spanish-born jazz pianist who had run an under-graduate group known as the Quinquaginta Ramblers and had managed to get it recorded on Brunswick, was appointed band-leader of an all-star group to play at the Savoy. It has been said that the recordings made by this group, which included many of the best American jazz performers, were undoubtedly the finest made in England during the decade.

The 1920s *did* see the emergence of genuine jazz, but it was a muted appearance. To the public at large jazz remained loud, raucous, and basically comical. It would be a long time before jazz ceased to be associated with trombones played with the feet and funny business with the drums.

CHAPTER FOUR

THE DANCE REVOLUTION

ALTHOUGH THERE WERE still old-fashioned dance bands, the emphasis throughout the 1920s was on providing dance music for the young. The traditional bands called themselves Hungarian or Viennese bands, though all the personnel were British. At one dance one of the 'foreigners' was approached with the idea of making him feel at home. 'Ah, you Hungary, eh?' the dancer asked slowly. 'You bet—and damned thirsty', riposted the musician. One of the bands playing at the Savoy, a plum engagement for itinerant musicians, was the New Savoy Tango Band, the members of which were dressed in national costume—coloured aprons, high-heeled boots with 'jewels' set in the heels, and black leather belts garnished with gold coins. To counter the phoney European bands the J. H. Squire Celeste Octet was founded. A new feature of the scene was the all-women dance band, one of which was Irene Davies's Dance Band.

A number of pre-war dances had survived the war. The most important of the new walking dances, the predecessor of the fox-trot, was the Boston, but after immense popularity during 1910–11 this died in 1914. The tango remained in vogue, clearly seen in the number of tango bands that did the circuit of the hotels, but a dance that promised to rival it, the maxixe, did not stay the course, though it was eventually disinterred as the samba. During the Edwardian period the waltz had been slowed right down, and only amongst purists was the old-fashioned Viennese

Many bands gave themselves exotic foreign titles; William Russell's London Bohemian Band played safe (Harry Mortimer)

waltz danced. The waltz continued to form a large slice of the music played at formal dances. In 1924 the dancing establishment agreed on two forms of fox-trot as basic dances; the faster was eventually called the quickstep.

Writing in the mid-1920s, the novelist Alec Waugh, brother of Evelyn, looked at the changing face of dancing:

> When we went as small children to a kintergarden dancing class, we were taught the polka and the waltz, the lancers and the Highland fling. There were on the average programme some seven or eight different dances. Today there are only fox-trots, and an occasional waltz, with here and there a tango for the exhibitionists.

He considered that dancing for dancing's sake was a thing of the past; it was no longer the dance that mattered, but the place where one went to dance and he computed that nine-tenths of the average person's dancing took place in restaurant, hotel, and night club.

In every big restaurant there was dancing. After coffee the carpet was rolled away, the trays of sweets wheeled back against the wall, and the band began to play, lethargic or frenetic depending on circumstances. Another innovation was the cabaret, which followed the dinner-dance.

In its twentieth-century sense, the term 'cabaret' was introduced in 1915, but it was only after the war that the craze started in New York restaurants, with dancing-space, and roomy platforms which could be moved about the place. On these a comedian would do his act, novelty musicians performed their specialities, and pretty girls displayed their charms. The shows were timed to begin about midnight, when the New York theatres had closed, and proved immensely popular amongst the post-war jaded and the post-prandial roués.

It was not long before the cabaret came to London, establishing itself during the winter of 1921–2, and it became a feature of restaurant, dance-club and perhaps the most characteristic of 1920s entertainments, the night-club. These categories often merged into one another, and even infringed on intimate revue at the Cave of Harmony in Charlotte Street, intellectual titillation for the Bloomsburyites. There was nothing of West End swish about the Cave of Harmony, two dingy rooms divided by a hall. In the smaller of the rooms was a bar and tables, while the larger was a studio with a ricketty stage, on which, occasionally, plays by Pirandello and Huxley were acted. Every third Saturday was

Every important hotel and restaurant had its orchestra, and so did many of the big stores, such as Harrod's (Wonderful London)

It was the age of the dance-club, the night-club, and cabaret
(Wonderful London)

a riotous fancy-dress ball. To its habitués the Cave of Harmony was cabaret, and the West End opposition mere usurpers.

The fashion for dance-clubs was started before World War I, and American ragtime musicians often made their debuts in them. One was Bert Earle, who 'put such vigour and rhythm into his playing of the banjo that he gave new zest to dancing. All sorts of people who had felt bewildered trying to dance the old-fashioned waltz and the seductive gliding "Boston" were tempted to go on the floor and foot it to the strains of "On the Mississippi", "Snookey-Ookums", and "Alexander's Rag-Time Band." '

One of the leading dance-clubs of the immediate pre-war period was the Cosmopolitan, run by Jack May who had had experience of similar places in New York, and he was so successful that he founded Murray's Club in Beak Street, the first of the restaurant-dance-clubs, which featured gala nights with elaborate gifts to lady members, introduced the 'thé dansant', and pioneered an innovation that was to prove immensely popular in the post-war years—exhibition dances by professionals. It was this more than anything that brought in the Charleston and the Black Bottom.

The dance-clubs were orientated to the upper and middle classes. The Four Hundred Club in Bond Street was initially entitled The Public Schools and Universities Dance Club, and a tie-up was effected between the club and the Savoy Hotel. The first luxury dance-club was Ciro's, formed by Clement Hobson who had recently acquired the renowned Ciro's Restaurant in Monte Carlo. He lamented that because of quaint licensing laws London was prevented from having a restaurant on the lines of his Monte Carlo restaurant or the Café de Paris, Paris. The only way to get round this was to form a club which, under club law, could remain open until 2 am. Ciro's took on the recognised restaurants at their own game, and employed a seven-piece black band at the then sensational salary of £100 a week.

The pre-war dance-clubs were not considered a significant phenomenon. Ciro's re-opened in 1919, the Four Hundred Club was renamed the Embassy and was for a time run by Albert de Courville who had pioneered spectacular revue at the London Hippodrome, the Ambassador opened in Conduit Street, and in November 1922 the Metropole came along, frequented by the then Prince of Wales (later Edward VIII). Despite trouble with the London County Council, which required the number of performers to be limited to six and put a ban on scenery and costumes, late-night entertainment was no longer the prerogative of the dissipated who would be much better occupied elsewhere.

Perhaps the most spectacular of the dinner and dance clubs was the Kit-Cat Club, with the largest dancing area of any club in London and an enormous balcony where people could dine and look on. The cream of talent, American and British played there, including Paul Whiteman's Band and Jack Hylton's Band. So did Sophie Tucker, and it was the dance-club most favoured by visiting American tourists. Not all were appreciative of this form of amusement; in May 1925 Arnold Bennett visited the Kit-Cat Club:

> To see this space crammed with dancers who could only sway to and fro to hear the row of the Vincent Lopez £1,100 a week band from New York, and other lower noises—gave you the impression that the bottom had fallen out of civilization.

A statuette of a dancer, no more exotic than the real thing (Sotheby & Co)

To men like Bennett the large sums paid out to bands and entertainers were as reprehensible and disgusting as the music and the dancing. He had been appalled in 1923 when he went to the Savoy to hear the Savoy Orpheans, twelve musicians who 'play strange instruments all looking like silver and gold. The piano has two manuals and a harpsichord attachment . . . they played bad music well . . . Count G. "finest saxophone player in the world" . . . paid £83 per week . . . band cost £430–£460 a week'. The cost of the bands at the Piccadilly Hotel was £68,000 a year and the fees for speciality dancers, singers, and entertainers accounted for another £32,000. In 1927 the bandleader Ambrose crossed from the Embassy Club to the Mayfair Hotel, a personal salary of £10,000 a year making him the best-paid bandleader in the world. At the Kit-Cat, Teddy Brown's band was being paid £1,000 a week.

There was big money in cabaret, dance-club, and night-club. In one week in 1924 the Piccadilly Cabaret took £1,900, a figure that vied with the box-office receipts of musical comedy hits. Luigi Naintré bought the Embassy for £6,000 and sold it two years later to a syndicate for £42,000, remaining as managing director. In five years the restaurant turnover amounted to £645,000.

Just as there was spectacular and intimate revue, so there were spectacular and intimate dance-clubs, one of the latter being Chez Victor in Grafton Street where, like the Cave of Harmony, the atmosphere being projected was likened to that of a house party. The money to be made from parting rich diner-dancers from their money resulted in a crop of clip-joints, operating under the name of night-clubs, where sparkling wine was substituted for champagne and painted hostesses danced with semi-intoxicated men. These formed a parallel to the American 'barrelhouses', hotbeds of earthy jazz and boogie-woogie. Perhaps the music played in the more unsavoury night-clubs had something of the dash and vigour of their American counterparts.

Ostensibly, dance clubs were not confined to the well-to-do, and the London Club was opened just off Baker Street, the brain-child of Tom Gordon, a billiard-hall tycoon. The London

Club had a membership of about 10,000, and as many as 1,000 people at a time would drink, dine, and dance at prices that the lower-middle classes could afford. The London Club was celebrated as a great breakthrough in giving the less rich the benefits of new entertainment forms, but as Mr Gordon originally planned to use the site for a permanent circus it would seem that he made the best of a bad job. As well as a cabaret show on West End models there were forty billiard tables.

The London Club was not directed at the great mass of Londoners, and the fact that vintage wine was seven shillings a bottle cheaper than in the West End clubs would have cut little ice with a £2-a-week labouring man. For the young dancing proletariat there were dance halls moulded hopefully on the Hammersmith Palais, but generally speaking the workers were not encouraged to join in the fun-loving world of debs, flappers and their escorts.

By the end of 1924 there were about a dozen cabarets in the West End, with supper and entertainment all-in at prices from £1 to £2 per head. These were eminently respectable, well attended, and, wrote 'Quex' (G. H. Fosdike Nichols) of the *Evening News*, 'I have seen the Duke of Westminster, and even imperious stage beauties, compelled to wait at the entrance for tables'. Night-clubs came and went, raided and closed down by the police, to re-open again under different names. There was a considerable amount of drug trafficking in the night-clubs.

In the smoky, heavily-perfumed atmosphere of the dance-clubs it was often difficult to breathe, let alone dance, and the floors were so crowded that even a fox-trot was slowed down to something approaching a funeral march. It was therefore surprising when dance-clubs became the breeding-ground of the floor-consuming short-skirt dances that are forever associated with the 1920s, particularly the Charleston. These were first given an airing by professional dance teams, the doyen of these dancers being Irene Castle who officiated at the Embassy. The agile customers who wished to avail themselves of the opportunities were taught at specialised dancing schools where the intricacies of slaps, pick-ups, pull-backs and triples were explained.

The popularity of new dances did not displace the tango

It is often supposed that the Charleston summed up the twenties, but in reality it was a craze that lasted only two years. Athletic, exhibitionist, and asexual, it was danced only by a minority. As an expression of living for kicks and a reaction against post-war *ennui* it brought in shoals of letters from irate colonels and enraged chartered accountants and provided copy for newspapers. A hotel that barred the Charleston received extravagant publicity.

But, as *Punch* said, the Charleston 'may not always be intentional. It may be that the girl has been freshly shingled that day, and some of the clipped hairs are causing irritation down her back'. Shingling was more typical of the age than the Charleston.

The god of the 1920s was novelty, whether it was in art, serious music, dance music and jazz, architecture or literature.

The Charleston (Punch)

It was the age of Surrealism, *Façade* and James Joyce, as well as saxophones. Novelty for novelty's sake had the seeds of disintegration already sprouting, and when a craze was on a downward trend there were few to fight for it. Even Tin Pan Alley, which owed its existence to the pursuit of the new, did not want to know, and disclaimed all knowledge of such trite phenomena. When the Black Bottom displaced the Charleston the copywriters licked their pencils and started again.

There were outsiders who saw through the whole of the charade, such as C. L. Graves who mocked the whole scene in the style of Swinburne:

> And agile maidens, dainty and dapper,
>   Sleeker of head than the orb of the plum,
> Each with her chosen whipper-snapper,
>   Forth to the fox-trot nightly come;
> And above the chatter of midnight meals
>   The cornet bleats and the saxo squeals,
> And the sandalled hoofs of the fearless flapper
>   Follow the beat of the furious drum.

Not all were taken in by High Life in London.

CHAPTER FIVE

TIN PAN ALLEY

TIN PAN ALLEY is concerned with the promotion and marketing of popular music, and took its name from 28th Street, the American equivalent of Denmark Street the narrow lane running from Charing Cross Road to St. Giles's High Street.

The 1920s were a busy time for Tin Pan Alley, for the concept of popular music was being extended, and the gramophone and the wireless were factors that had to be taken into account, as well as the outpouring of American music, the rights in which were eagerly taken up by British music-publishing companies. With the coming of talkies in 1928, film rights needed to be considered.

The money from popular music was being radically re-distributed, and the days were long gone when a composer depended for his income on the sales of sheet music. As early as 1922 the sharp decline in the sales of sheet music had been noted. There were a number of reasons for this, one being the impact of the gramophone. Previously, if anyone wished to hear a popular music-hall song in the home it was necessary to buy the music and perform it oneself. Now a prospective performer could listen to the gramophone record, and copy it. Although people still gave musical evenings, at which amateur singers and instrumentalists attended and gave of their best, it was now very much a declining habit; it was far simpler to wind up the gramophone and put on a record, and with the immense variety of records available there was no area where a lacuna existed. There were music-hall and variety songs, mournful ballads, and instrumental solos in abundance. The girl who took her harp to the party would rarely have been asked to play.

Sheet music sales also took a knock because of the popularity of the self-playing piano, the Pianola and its contemporaries. Although the player-piano never achieved the immense success it did in the United States, there were many thousands of them about, and the piano-roll publishers put their rolls on to the market as quickly as the publishers put sheet music. The piano rolls of popular songs were printed with the words; as the roll wound over the spools the appropriate lyrics were displayed to view, and a singer had the inestimable advantage that he or she had an accompanist that was considerably better than the usual amateur pianist, lack the personal touch though it did.

Among the popular song rolls issued in 1927 were Irving Berlin's 'Because I love you', Henderson's 'Black bottom' (cashing in on the new dance), Ager's 'Lay me down to sleep in Carolina', Myers's 'Moonlight on the Ganges', Russell's 'Memories of you', 'Rosie-Posie's waltz', Tilzer's 'My cutie's due at ten-to-two today', Stone's 'Perhaps you'll think of me', and Longstaffe's 'When the sergeant-major's on parade'. A belated effort to join in the community-singing boom was provided by a pianist named Frank Stanton whose roll of community-song choruses comprised 'Pack up your troubles', 'Love's old sweet song', and 'Tipperary'.

From the quantity of song rolls that are found today in antique and junk shops it is certain that they were widely sold, and unquestionably player-pianos were a feature in the houses of those who had done well out of the war, as much a status symbol as expensive gramophones and wireless sets. The average music-lover made do with less expensive equipment. Gramophones could be bought for as little as £2, whereas a player-piano from Keith Prowse started at £116.

In 1914 the Performing Rights Society was formed, and in 1924 its president, William Boosey of Chappell's, predicted that Performing Rights fees would be the composers' biggest, and

In the old days, a singer could identify with a song for months or even years. The wireless and the gramophone finished this. An engraving by Walter Sickert (Courtesy Victoria and Albert Museum)

perhaps only, source of income. This statement was pooh-poohed as alarmist talk, but the figures were to speak for themselves. In 1925 sales of sheet music totalled £566,459, in 1929 they were down to £453,564, and in 1933 they had slumped to £284,691. The days were gone when Ivor Novello could sit down, write 'Keep the home fires burning', and be better off to the tune of £16,000.

The drop in sheet-music sales also reflected the decline of the music hall and the coming of broadcasting. In the old days a singer could identify himself with a song and sing it for months and even years at music halls. Every time he sang it there were a dozen potential sheet-music buyers in the stalls. A song on the wireless could reach more people in a night, even in 1924, than could ever hear it in the flesh; and the listeners did not rush away to buy the music. Why should they? If they liked the song they would go and buy the record. The wireless was the great populariser, and this was taken into account by the Performing Rights Society; owners of a copyright song received an appointed share of the money paid out by the BBC on account of copyright fees. The Performing Rights Society, acting for about 40,000 composers, collected payments for broadcasting on the basis of 5½d each for the first million licensed listeners, 4½d for the second million, 3½d for the third, and 3¼d thereafter. With 2 million licence-holders (not listeners) this worked out at approximately £25,000 a year, which was allotted on a 'points' basis. A dance tune got one point every time it was performed, and so on up the scale to seven points for a symphonic work. Few composers were able to get rich on this, and when it is considered that one record firm in the year 1928–9 made a net profit of £1 million the money doled out by the BBC was parsimonious—2½ per cent of its licence income.

Nevertheless the picture was not all black, and what a composer lost on the swings he made up on the roundabouts, literally— gramophone rights. Gramophone royalties went up from £134,220 in 1925 to £296,871 in 1929. And one source of income remained stable—the pantomime. Music halls might go and British musical comedies collapse in the American invasion, but the pantomime was part of the British way of life, and many famous songs were written especially for the pantomime market, being slipped in no matter what the context. In the pantomime season 1925–6 *Goody Two Shoes* playing at the Theatre Royal, Nottingham, incorporated 'Sunny Havana', 'Why don't my dreams come true?', 'Save your sorrow', and 'When my sugar walks in the street'. *Humpty Dumpty* at the Theatre Royal, Glasgow, had as its hit number 'I've never wronged an onion'.

Popular songs were relentlessly promoted using modern methods of advertising, and if there were possible tie-ups the music publishers left no stones unturned. Unusual and novelty songs were best-suited to this treatment, and in 1923 'Yes, we have no bananas' was publicised by giving away free bananas. The banana importers Elders & Fyffes donated £500 for the publicity given to them, and whole-page spreads were taken in the trade journals to push this song. It was so successful that there was a follow-up in 1926, 'I've never seen a straight banana', and £1,000 was offered by the Denmark Street publishers to anyone who could produce a perfectly straight one. This stunt backfired, for the offices were beleaguered by hundreds of hopefuls. In the end, no absolutely straight banana was found, and a prize was given to the least curly.

The publishers of 'Me and Jane in a plane' (1927) publicised it by hiring a plane containing the Jack Hylton band, and 'Souvenirs' was advertised on the front page of the *Daily Mail*. The full-page spread cost £1,450 but the song netted £20,000, so the publishers, Lawrence Wright, were happy, especially as the composer *was* Lawrence Wright alias Horatio Nicholls, a prolific producer of 600 songs including 'That old fashioned mother of mine'.

Lawrence Wright used Blackpool as a touchstone. If a song did well in Blackpool it would be a popular success. But Wright was not parochial, and he appreciated the growing interest in American music, signing up the veteran Walter Donaldson, composer of 'Georgia' (1922), 'Let it rain, let it pour' (1925), 'I wonder where my baby is tonight' (1925) and 'My blue heaven' (1927), for the then phenomenal sum of $30,000. Although there were song-writers who worked hard at their job, many of them boasted how little it had cost them to write a best-seller. 'Shepherd of the hills' was written on the transatlantic telephone (at a charge of £150), and 'Wyoming' by Horatio Nicholls, dashed off in a few minutes, was heard by the musical director of the Palace Theatre, Herman Finck, who liked it and pushed it, and it sold 3 million copies. What sheet music did sell sold in abundance.

The old-stagers who had been purveying ballads since the beginning of time were out of step with the new methods of

A 1926 hit, Red red robin, *sung by Whispering Jack Smith*

Tin Pan Alley, though they, too, had been commercially promoted at 'Royalty' concerts where they had a share of the take for singing the ballads of the publishers who had hired the hall. But no matter how they sneered at commercialism they took care to keep their names in the papers and were always willing to provide copy. 'I have sung many hundreds of songs during my career', said Dame Clara Butt in 1926, 'and I do not think I have sung any bad ones . . . I have never grown tired of singing "Abide with me" . . . What we need is more songs like "The lost chord". There is something of the grandeur of Beethoven in it.' The image was somewhat tarnished when Clara Butt, now fifty-seven, set off to Australia for a concert tour. 'Sing 'em muck', advised Dame Nellie Melba, 'it's all they can understand'.

Stars of opera and the concert hall were not averse to cashing in on personal publicity. The singer Tetrazzini announced that her pets included fifteen dogs, five cats, two peacocks, and a tiger called 'Poosy', and she had her photograph taken nursing a young crocodile. In a newspaper interview she also gave advice to tyro singers: 'Do not attack a note at the same time that you are inhaling. That is too soon.' Gigli bragged about his sixty bedroom castle, and was proud of the fact that he travelled with two secretaries, two valets, and eleven other attendants. The pianist de Pachmann (1848–1933) was as well known for his rudeness and boastfulness as for his playing: 'Once there were two pianists in the world. They were Liszt and Pachmann. Liszt is dead.' At a concert in Portsmouth in 1923 he pointed to a man in the audience, and screamed, 'He is not in sympathy with Chopin, and I should be glad if he would leave!' And how his audiences loved it (all except the unfortunate man singled out for the benefit of the Pachmann legend). Even the most publicity-mad jazz musicians would have hesitated before trying that gambit out, though there was a note of insouciance in Jack Hylton's comment that 'Sir Edward Elgar's type of composition is, of course, very different from mine'.

Jack Hylton and the other leading conductors such as Jack Payne, who was one of the first to have a show band which did the rounds of the circuit variety theatres, could afford to take this tone, for despite the visits of Paul Whiteman and his symphonic jazz band there was no question that British bands were supreme. Occasionally Hylton's preoccupation with the money he was making backfired:

> Jack Hylton, the jazz king of the British Isles, says he's been offered 5,000 dollars a week to take his band to New York. Some people are asking him if the offer did not originate in the British Isles.

With composers it was another matter, for it was clear to all that the pre-eminence that British and European composers enjoyed until World War I had been shattered. It is interesting to look at the popular songs written by Americans in the 1920s, to realise that they were directed at a public ill-served by Noel Coward and Vivian Ellis. British popular composers were still catering for a middle-class audience, and most of them were unwilling or unable to tackle the mass market with the classless gusto of the Americans:

Milton Ager:	'I'm nobody's baby', 1921
	'Ain't she sweet?', 1927
Fred Ahlert:	'I'll get by', 1928
	'Mean to me', 1930
Harry Akst:	'Dinah', 1925
	'Baby face', 1926
Abel Baer:	'I ain't got nobody', 1928
Irving Berlin:	'Say it with music', 1920
	'Three cheers for the red, white and blue', 1922
	'What'll I do?', 1924
	'All alone', 1924
	'Always', 1925
	'Blue skies', 1927
	'Russian lullaby', 1927
	'The song is ended', 1927
Nacio Herb Brown:	'Broadway melody', 1929
	'Singing in the rain', 1929
	'You were meant for me', 1929
	'Pagan love song', 1929

Joe Burke:	'Tip-toe through the tulips', 1929
	'Painting the clouds with sunshine', 1929
Hoagy Carmichael:	'Star dust', 1929
Con Conrad:	'Margie', 1920
	'Ma, he's making eyes at me', 1921
Will Marion Cook:	'I'm coming, Virginia', 1926
Walter Donaldson:	'Carolina in the morning', 1922
	'Georgia', 1922
	'Let it rain, let it pour', 1925
	'Yes, sir, that's my baby', 1925
	'I wonder where my baby is tonight', 1925
	'After I say I'm sorry', 1926
	'My blue heaven', 1927
	'Making whoopee', 1928
Ted Fiorito:	'When lights are low', 1924
	'Laugh, clown, laugh', 1928
Fred Fisher:	'Chicago', 1922
	'Ich liebe dich', 1929
George Gershwin:	'I'll build a stairway to paradise', 1922
	'Somebody loves me', 1924
	'The man I love', 1924
	'Lady be good', 1924
	'Fascinating rhythm', 1924
	'That certain feeling', 1925
	'Someone to watch over me', 1926
	'Clap yo' hands', 1926
	'S'wonderful', 1927
	'Feeling I'm falling', 1928
	'Liza', 1929
Ray Henderson:	'Birth of the blues', 1925
	'Five foot two, eyes of blue', 1925
	'Bye, bye, blackbird', 1926
	'The best things in life are free', 1927
	'Sonny boy', 1928
	'Button up your overcoat', 1929
	'My lucky star', 1929
	'I'm a dreamer, aren't we all?', 1929
	'If I had a talking picture of you', 1929
	'Keep your sunny side up', 1929
Jerome Kern:	'Sally', 1920
	'Look for the silver lining', 1920
	'Who', 1925
	'Ol' man river', 1927

	'Can't help lovin' that man', 1927
	'Why do I love you?', 1927
	'Make believe', 1927
Jimmy McHugh:	'I can't give you anything but love', 1928
Cole Porter:	'Let's do it', 1928
	'You do something to me', 1929
	'What is this thing called love?', 1929
J. Russell Robinson:	'Margie', 1920
Richard Rodgers:	'Manhattan', 1925
	'Here in my arms', 1925
	'Mountain greenery', 1926
	'Blue room', 1926
	'My heart stood still', 1927
	'You took advantage of me', 1928
	'With a song in my heart', 1929
Sigmund Romberg:	'Deep in my heart', 1924
	'Serenade' (from *The Student Prince*, 1924)
	'The desert song', 1926
	'One alone', 1926
	'Softly, as in a morning sunrise', 1928
	'Lover, come back to me', 1928
Sammy Stept:	'That's my weakness now', 1928
Henry Sullivan:	'I may be wrong but I think you're wonderful', 1929
Fats Waller:	'Ain't misbehavin' ', 1929
Mabel Wayne:	'In a little Spanish town', 1926
	'Ramona', 1927
Richard Whiting:	'Ain't we got fun?', 1921
	'Sleepy time gal', 1924
	'She's funny that way', 1928
Harry Woods:	'When the red, red robin', 1926
	'I'm looking over a four-leaf clover', 1927
Vincent Youmans:	'Oh me, oh my, oh you', 1921
	'Deep in my heart', 1924
	'I want to be happy', 1925
	'Tea for two', 1925
	'I know that you know', 1926
	'Sometimes I'm happy', 1927
	'Hallelujah', 1927
	'Great day', 1929
	'Without a song', 1929
	'Time on my hands', 1929

It will be readily seen that the American popular-song composers did not have the British coyness and hesitation about love songs; some of them were frankly sex songs. In British songs there was an assumption that lovers were either engaged or married, but there was none of this prevarication by the Americans, and their robust attitude was both welcomed and deprecated, and Tin Pan Alley had to be wary in pushing the more unequivocal songs.

The essential quality about American popular songs was that they were white men's music, and it was rare for a negro composer/ executant like Fats Waller to make an impression on the wider market. Not that there are any shortages of negro topics; when a love song was unusually explicit it was assigned to black people, commonly supposed to be fun-loving and untrammelled by convention. An interesting feature of the above list is the number of composers either of European descent or new arrivals in the United States; perhaps they could isolate the specifically important elements of popular song that made them best-sellers.

Today it would be idle to deny any of this select list merit, but at the time the tunes were inextricably bound up with the mythology of jazz (unseemly, indecorous, unclean, etc etc). In his book *Music Ho!* Constant Lambert viciously attacked the 1920s popular song, comparing it with the pre-war model, where 'a general air of physical attractiveness, sexual bounce and financial independence is naturally assumed. . . . In modern songs [he was writing in 1933] it is taken for granted that one is poor, unsuccessful, and either sex-starved or unable to hold the affections of such partner as one may have had the luck to pick up'. He selected 'Ain't misbehavin' ' and 'When you want somebody who don't want you, perhaps you'll think of me' as examples of the modern song.

But Lambert also lambasted 'the series of crazy words, crazy tune numbers, with their assumed galvanic energy', and went on to say that the most irritating quality about the 'Vo-dodeo-vo, poop-a-poop school of jazz song is its hysterical emphasis on the fact that the singer is a jazz baby going crazy about jazz rhythms'. Like many of his contemporaries Lambert was giving in to his prejudices, which were racial rather than musical: 'the fact that at least ninety per cent of jazz tunes are written by Jews undoubtedly goes far to account for the curiously sagging quality—so typical of Jewish art—the almost masochistic melancholy of the average foxtrot'. Lambert's dashing style cannot prevent one seeing that he wanted it both ways and twisted facts to suit his purposes. He represented a mentality that waged war on Tin Pan Alley for providing an article that was indescribably awful, and accused it of being a commercialised Wailing Wall.

Without American imports, Tin Pan Alley would have been in a parlous state. In dealing with home products it had no idea what constituted a bestseller, why acres of publicity could fail to win public interest and yet unconsidered trifles could rocket. Why did fourteen record companies fall over themselves to record 'The tin can fusiliers'? Predictably 'Tea for two' was the most recorded tune of 1926, but which panjandrum could have picked out number two in the charts? Who would have believed that this was 'The toy drum major', recorded 32 times, and selling 956,784 records?

CHAPTER SIX

THE GRAMOPHONE

IN THE YEARS prior to World War I America went dance crazy, and one-steps, Bostons, and ragtime records poured from the presses. One of the two leading firms, Victor, engaged Vernon and Irene Castle to supervise the making of all its dance records. The Castles were the nation's leading authorities on ballroom dancing, and in the 1920s after the death of her husband Irene Castle was a leading figure in the popularisation of new dances in London dance-clubs.

The expiration of gramophone and phonograph patents meant that dozens of companies were joining in the battle for the public's money, and talking machines of all shapes and sizes came on to the market. The Vocalion 'Art Models' ranged in price from $375 to $2,000 (£75–£400 at the rate of exchange then), and prospective purchasers were urged to consider that they were not buying an article of the calibre of a furnace or a laundry tub but an 'outward and visible sign of inward and spiritual grace'. The aim was to make a gramophone look as little like one as possible.

The Americans were not much interested in classical records; Edison, whose new 'disc phonograph' of 1913 was better than any other recorder on the market, was proud of the fact that his favourite song was 'I'll take you home again, Kathleen'. Serious music was left to the Europeans, and the war years saw a rejection of celebrity vocalists in favour of the coming men of orchestral

Sir Thomas Beecham was one of the principal
opponents of the gramophone, but he did not
hesitate to make recordings when the
opportunity arose (Raphael)

and instrumental music, especially Sir Henry Wood and Sir
Thomas Beecham. Although Beecham was never happier than
when slating the gramophone, that did not stop him making
records.

Nevertheless the British branch of Columbia realised that there
were enormous pickings in popular music, and shortly after the
war Columbia signed up the principals of every successful revue
in London, the records of whom sold well and enabled the
company to plough money into a classical catalogue. It was a
grand gesture, but nothing could disguise the truncation and
mutilation, with Henry Wood compressing Dukas's *The
Sorcerer's Apprentice* and Wagner's *Flying Dutchman* overture into
less than eight minutes. HMV joined in, signing up Elgar and

Edward German to conduct their own works, while Columbia probed cautiously into the mysteries of chamber music, and by the early 1920s there were few fields of music untouched.

For music in a lighter vein there was 'The jigger jag' played by the Aeolian Orchestra, an unknown studio band, 'The vamp' played by the Banjovials Novelty Dance Orchestra, 'Bo-la-bo' by the Black Diamonds Band, and 'He'd say Oo la-la wee-wee' by the Blackpool Tower Orchestra. Many companies had their own bands. The Black Diamonds Band was the military-style house band of the Zonophone Company, and the London Orchestra was an HMV band, as was the Mayfair Dance Orchestra. The description 'Royal Military Band' was applied to a number of gramophone-company house bands.

In 1923 the magazine *The Gramophone* brought order into confusion, and Frank Swinnerton, the novelist, wrote an article in it in defence of the gramophone. To some 'it is an infernal machine which makes all music sound as if it were being played by nursery soldiers'. He complained that the recording of an orchestra always had a tinny vibration, and that the piano resembled the banjo. His main quarrel was with the limitations of the 12in disc which meant that music had to be ruthlessly cut, though he admitted that needles hissed less and there was less crackle than was once the case.

By 1923 acoustic recording was as good as it could be made; a full symphony orchestra could be recorded without dodges such as replacing the double bass with a tuba, but the process remained limited to a range of 168–2,000 cycles (a range of 20–20,000 cycles is audible in the concert hall). This did not necessarily cut out notes, but it did alter the tone and timbre, not noticed in popular music but very evident in serious music.

The intention of giving the public a goodly ration of decent music was carried out by the gramophone companies and the wireless, and by 1924 works as advanced as Holst's *The Planets* and Stravinsky's *Petrouchka* were on record. It was curious that the first British symphony on record was the obscure Solway Symphony by McEwen, though Vaughan Williams's London Symphony entered the lists in the same year (omitting a movement now and then). The first string quartet to be recorded in its entirety was Brahms's opus 51 no 1, put on disc in 1923.

A good deal of snobbishness permeated those circles where decisions were made on what gramophone records were to be put on the market or what programmes were to be broadcast. It was still considered that 'They' knew best what the public ought to have, and even what it wanted, and there was little communication between the top brass of radio and gramophone companies and Tin Pan Alley, whose rough-and-ready sampling gave inklings that the taste of the masses was a good deal grubbier than they were given credit for being.

Consequently, when duties towards British contemporary music and high-flying operatic singers were completed, a considerable amount of middlebrow music found its way on to the market, typified by a bestseller that was to be found in radio request programmes well into the 1940s, Purcell's 'Nymphs and shepherds' sung by a choir of Manchester schoolchildren. Just as remarkable was 'Hear my prayer', a 1926 record featuring Ernest Lough, the boy soprano, with the Temple Church Choir and George Thalben-Ball as choirmaster and organist. This record, number C1329, earned so much money that a scholarship was financed by the royalties.

The gramophone business in Britain had been founded on middle-of-the-road operatic arias sung by expensive celebrities, and the old habits died hard. The 24-year-old Polish singer Kiepura was offered a £1,000 a year contract, and played one company against another, each of them frenziedly bidding for a potential Caruso. Afterwards it was found that Kiepura was just another singer. The promotion of operatic arias by gramophone companies led to their being accepted as examples of popular music, and they found their way into the everyman repertoire. As instrumental solos came out well on early records, these too were relentlessly pushed, and violinists of the middle rank were able to claim enormous fees. When his contract with Victor ran out, Fritz Kreisler signed another guaranteeing him $750,000 over five years. It did not signify that his popularity was based on a clutch of salon pieces which he claimed had been composed by early composers, but were in reality written by himself, and it is pleasant to turn to a great pianist getting a smash hit—Wilhelm Backhaus with the 'Naila' waltz by Delibes coupled with Liszt's 'Liebestraume No 3', which sold a quarter of a million copies.

This was comforting to the gramophone record companies, for a very real opposition to records of pianists existed in piano rolls made by famous pianists. In one month alone rolls were published (with a running commentary) of Percy Grainger playing the first movement of Grieg's piano concerto, Harold Bauer playing Chopin's 'Revolutionary' study, Artur Rubinstein playing Manuel de Falla's 'Ritual Fire Dance', Busoni playing Liszt's 'La Campanella', while the most advanced of *avant garde* music was being promoted with a zest that the gramophone companies might envy—Stravinsky playing his own piano sonata, Pouishnoff playing Scriabin, and Prokofiev performing his own 'Sarcasms'.

The piano-roll companies, especially Duo-Art and Aeolian, were also operating in the educational field, and if gramophone companies cast eyes at the popularity of wireless talks on music appreciation they also had to consider rolls such as 'Ear-training and rhythmic movements' by Mabel Chamberlain. Only the expense of good player-pianos kept lovers of piano music content with the hiss and crackle of shellac, for in every way player-pianos triumphed. In a book on the instrument Ernest Newman stated why:

> I have often heard pianoforte playing at a concert that, if I had not seen the pianist, I should have taken for a mediocre performance on a piano-player; and I have more than once heard, from behind a door, a piano-player performance that gave me no suspicion that a mechanical instrument was concerned in it.

The advantages of a player-piano (or piano-player) were rubbed home by Newman:

> As I write these lines, a young lady (I am sure it is a young lady!) in a house a few doors away is playing the finale of the 'Moonlight

Sonata' (with the windows open, of course, for the benefit of th
neighbours), as she has played it every morning for a fortnight
Every morning she is pulled up dead at the same place and has to
begin again; every morning she shows that she has no more idea
of Beethoven in her than a coal-heaver has of Keats . . . Had her
parents bought her a piano-player in her childhood, instead of
sending her to 'learn the piano', there might by now be a different
story to tell.

Newman also made the observation that as modern piano
music was approaching the unplayable except by one or two
virtuosos, much fine and adventurous music would only get a
hearing by means of the player-piano.

The 1920s saw the British taking an interest in the gramophone
as a piece of furniture. An article in *Our Homes and Gardens* in
1921 stated:

> In its original form the gramophone was not only very crude as a
> musical instrument, but also very unsightly, its horn especially
> being so aggressive that its presence in any room was regrettable,
> and in some rooms unthinkable . . . the gramophone now has not
> only established itself as a serious musical instrument capable of
> reproducing every kind of vocal and instrumental music with an
> astonishing degree of fidelity and charm, but equally it claims
> consideration as a piece of furniture which can be made to harmonise
> with any scheme.

Fine cabinet makers were brought on to the scene, and a model
such as the 'Duncan Phyfe: Fulton' would, indeed, grace any
room. Unfortunately for the house-proud and genteel producers
of schemes, the gramophone was to be drastically refashioned for
the needs of electrical recording.

An electromechanical recorder had been designed and patented
as early as 1903 but had to await the invention of the condensor
microphone and vacuum-tube amplifier before the possibilities
could be realised. Two British technicians began work on the
problem in 1919, and in 1920 recorded the Armistice Day service
in Westminster Abbey using electrical means. It was the first
recording made using a remote pick-up, the sound being

The NEW Gramophone Invention all the Press is talking about

The New
COLUMBIA GRAFONOLA
Sir Henry J. Wood says

"I consider this instrument the greatest contribution to the advancement of music since the original invention of the gramophone itself."

Now announced for the first time, the New Columbia Grafonola is a revolution in tone, quality and volume. It is covered by exclusive patents. A triumph of British science and genius.

The New Record Invention

section Shows Columbia Patent Laminated Process

COLUMBIA *New Process* RECORDS
NO SCRATCH! PURE MUSIC!
NO SURFACE NOISES.

The most wonderful improvement in records since the beginning — pure music unmarred by needle scratch or surface noises.

The New Columbia Grafonola is produced in nineteen beautiful models from £5 10s. to £85. Write for Art Catalogue with 136-page Catalogue of Records, and name of nearest dealer, COLUMBIA, 102-108, Clerkenwell Road, London, E.C.1.

It was the aim of manufacturers to turn the gramophone into a handsome piece of furniture, and they sometimes succeeded
(Ideal Home)

transmitted over telephone to the recording machine outside the building. It impressed Columbia and HMV, and independently they began research into electric recording, if only to find out what the snags were and file a few patents to stop outsiders getting in. Neither company was particularly interested in setting up new equipment when the gramophone was doing very well as it was.

The American firm of Victor did not even bother about research, but a subsidiary of the rival American Telegraph and Telephone Company went into the matter. To reproduce properly the range of sound engraved by the electrical recording process, the horn of a mechanical gramophone needed to be 9ft long (an electrical gramophone had been built by American Telegraph but it was expensive to produce and subject to unforeseeable distortions). Manufacturers had a choice of folding the horn back on itself or making a feature of the monstrous trumpet; the Americans went for the first, making it possible to disguise the instrument as furniture, but the British favoured the long external horn.

Electrical recording meant that the frequency range had been extended to 100–5,000 cycles, that musicians no longer had to crouch around the microphone in discomfort but could spread themselves around a studio, and records had volume without blast. Gramophone companies with a big stake in acoustic records dithered, and it seemed more important to keep the public in the dark so that they would buy up the stock of old records rather than go ahead with the new system. Victor and Columbia agreed to keep quiet about electrical recording for a year, during which time retailers were urged to get rid of their stock of pre-electric gramophones and records. The 2nd of November 1925 was dubbed Victor Day, and American buyers rushed to buy, not quite knowing what except that it was different. Novelty in all things was a fetish of the 1920s.

The first electrical recordings were not announced as such in Britain, but it soon became apparent that something epoch-making had occurred. In England the first electrically recorded symphony—Tchaikovsky's Fourth—appeared in December 1925, and electric bestsellers from America, the dance number 'Let it rain, let it pour' and 'Adeste Fideles' sung by a 4,850-voice choir, made their appearance in the shops. 'Adeste Fideles' became a popular record through no very good reason except that it was peculiarly clear in texture, and it sold in Britain at the rate of 2,000 a day. The term 'electrical recording' was still taboo in Britain, and writers on the subject got round the difficulty with the term 'new recording'.

Because of the high quality of electrical recordings many companies thought that customers would not mind paying more for them. When everyone today laments the cost of living and the galloping consumption of inflation it is interesting to look back to the 1920s and see how much it cost music-lovers for their discs. Although Woolworth's were selling 7in records at 6d each, a double-sided 12in electrical recording of two La Scala extracts from Puccini's *Turandot* cost 6s 6d, while Elgar's Second Symphony, performed by the London Symphony Orchestra conducted by the composer, complete on six discs, cost nearly

The portable gramophone was a product of the new age (Ideal Home)

£2, well over £10 in present-day money. A gramophone could be bought for less than the Elgar symphony.

Record prices were in direct ratio to the prestige of the artists making them. In violin solos, Heifetz commanded 8s 6d a record, whereas the obscure Alfredo Rode was rated at 4s 6d; Pablo Casals was in the same bracket in cello records as Heifetz, but Cedric Sharpe was down in the bargain basement at 3s a throw.

Surprisingly, even those intimately connected with the world of the gramophone did not always appreciate the new electrical recordings. Compton Mackenzie, editor of *The Gramophone*, wrote:

> The exaggeration of sibilants by the new method is abominable, and there is a harshness which recalls some of the worst excesses of the past. The recording of massed strings is atrocious from an impressionistic standpoint. I don't want to hear symphonies with an American accent. I don't want blue-nosed violins and Yankee clarinets. I don't want the piano to sound like a free-lunch counter.

When he came to the recording of Tchaikovsky's Fourth Symphony he was opposed to the work itself as violently as he was to the rendering. It was, he declared, a jangle of shattered nerves. Readers of his magazine shared his sentiments, and it was not for another year that the ruffled feathers began to settle.

There were many who saw the gramophone as a modern usurper, eventually to kill live music, and the idea that it could be used in education was anathema. An interesting exchange of opinion took place in Westmorland, when a nationwide suspicion was voiced by members of the Kendal Town Council after a recommendation by the local education committee that a gramophone should be bought for the council school at a cost of £9 with records to the value of £5.

> COUNCILLOR ROBINSON: I really cannot see what gramophones have to do with education.
> COUNCILLOR BRAITHWAITE: It is just a fad on the part of two or three teachers in one particular school who are passionately fond of music. It looks to me like an insult to the pianoforte to put a gramophone in the same room. I am not a lover of tinned meat,

and am not a lover of tinned music. The two things compare very favourably in my eyes.

COUNCILLOR WEBB: We are told that the gramophone would be purchased to improve the education of the children—to differentiate between a Beethoven Sonata, a Chopin Waltz, and a Bach Fugue. If I put that question to the Council I should say that not three could make the differentiation. If that is so, I do not think a gramophone would be of any advantage to the school. It is time frittered away in that sort of thing.

There speak the massed voices of fuddy-duddy, and the conscious rejection of the new experiences opened by the widespread dissemination of the gramophone and its records. Essentially the two phenomena of gramophone and wireless had arrived too rapidly for old attitudes to be reshuffled. After they were established, things would never be the same again. Unquestionably more music was heard in the 1920s, music of all kinds, high-, middle- and lowbrow, than had been heard throughout all the previous history of mankind. It was not the mind-battering experience of later years with rock 'n roll and Muzac; but it was pervasive. Old Codgerdom could not keep up with it.

Although record critics gave most of their attention to the prestige works that were teeming from the record presses, they were obliged to cast a glance at the popular music. There were ballad revivals with Sullivan's 'Once again', and a nameless singer on the HMV label released 'two dreadful effusions', 'A little bit of heaven' and 'Mother Machree', sung by the Silver-Masked Tenor, and a singer named Walter Glynn plumbed the depths with 'Smilin' through' and 'Just because the violets'. There was also a vogue for 'whispering' singers. In the old days singers had tried their strength on 'The lost chord', but a new candidate had arrived to displace it, Oscar Rasbach's 'Trees' of 1922, which established roots that have still not been hacked away (though the song has proved to be a handy peg on which to hang a parody).

The astonishing quantity of the much-maligned shop ballads issued by the record companies makes it clear that there was still a demand for the lachrymose and the heart on the sleeve. These ballads were the staple fare of musical evenings, and as the records were only a few coppers apiece they were an inexpensive way of entertaining one's guests. The gramophone was a more social instrument than the wireless; except on the well-publicised ballad or light orchestral nights listeners never knew what to expect. Working out a gramophone programme made for personalised enjoyment, and the various formalities connected with putting on the records, winding the machine up, and changing the needles, gave guests the feeling that listening to the gramophone was as cosy as participating in a musical soirée. The gramophone recital was in for a rosy future.

Among the more popular of the ballads were Eric Coates's 'I hear you singing', Coningsby Clarke's 'The blind ploughman', the perennial Edward German's 'The Yeomen of England', Kennedy Russell's 'Poor man's garden', Teresa del Riego's 'Sink, red sun', and Besly's 'My bird of April days'. Song-writers hit by the decline in sheet-music sales still had the gramophone to count on; Fred Weatherly, who claimed 1,500 songs in all, produced the ultimate in front-parlour fodder with his new song, 'Danny boy'.

Common features of the shop or royalty ballads were that they dealt with aspects of life that had disappeared and sentiments that were second-hand and gathered from books of synonyms, used a restricted and predictable vocabulary, and were furbished with music that might be described in the terms of a critique of Margaret Sheridan, one of the first singers to record 'Danny boy' —pinched and wavering. The new lively popular songs of the American composers that since the ragtime age had threatened to sink the cliché-ridden for ever had not definitively triumphed. That the shop ballads were reviewed in the musical press, while Gershwin and Jerome Kern were contemptuously ignored, indicates that they were considered respectable. And respectability was highly valued in the musical establishment. A glance through the columns of gramophone notes demonstrates that what we take to be the characteristic features of the 1920s were not even acknowledged.

Novelty numbers had vied with operatic arias as suitable for early gramophones; because of eccentric and meretricious arranging there was little that they could be compared with. A record of an orchestral work could always be shown up against a live performance. Novelty numbers continued to be produced in quantity for unclassifiable buyers. 'A hunt in the Black Forest' was a hotchpotch of effects, with cocks crowing, birds twittering, horses galloping, and dogs barking. 'In a clock shop' was a medley of cuckoo-clocks, ticking, and clocks being wound and run down. Medvedov's Russian Balalaika Band was an incomprehensible jumble of jangling sound with the occasional 'Russian' cry of 'Ha!' The Grenadier Guards Band was involved in Eckersberg's 'Battle of Waterloo'. 'We are unmoved', wrote a critic, 'even when the entire British Army (numbering fully two dozen men) gives a couple of well-drilled cheers.' Even electrical recording was stumped by carillon solos, and one wonders who bought Columbia record 4510, 'Believe me, if all those endearing young charms' and 'Annie Laurie', played on the Ottawa Carillon at the Croydon Bell Foundry by Kamiel Lefèvre of Malines.

A class of composition allied to novelty numbers was that group of piano pieces that relied for their appeal on a kind of pseudo-ragtime quality, revamped 'Chopsticks'. One of the most prominent performers in this field was Zez Confrey who wrote a number of tunes in the 1920s—'Kitten on the keys' (1921), 'Stumbling' (1922), 'Dizzy fingers' (1923), and, a tribute to the coin-operated player-piano in pre-Prohibition American bars, 'Nickel in the slot' (1926). Not surprisingly, Americans such as Confrey were in the fore in this genre, but there were British players also, such as Max Darewski, later to be a well-known bandleader, and Melville Gideon, pianist with the Co-optimists, who recorded a ragtime improvisation in 1922 on Rubinstein's 'Melody in F'. Ernest Harrison recorded 'You tell 'em, ivories' in the same year, but perhaps the most prolific of the British syncopated players was Stanley C. Holt, who had led a dance band at the Savoy Hotel as early as 1915. In 1923 he recorded a clutch of numbers in the Zez Confrey manner, including 'Loose fingers', 'Piano puzzle', 'Coaxing the piano', 'Fidgety fingers',

'Rag man's exercise' and 'Cat's pyjamas'. Cecil Norman recorded 'Dustin' the keys', 'Tricky trix', and 'Dog on the piano', and Jean Panques was responsible for 'Flapperette' and 'Hot piano'.

Quite a number of musicians who were later to be important in the dance-band world started their careers as syncopated pianists. There was not only Darewski, but Jay Wilbur, and most of them seemed to want to play 'You tell 'em, ivories', which was recorded many times and was the lowbrow equivalent of Rachmaninoff's Prelude in C sharp minor, put on the middle-brow map by Mark Hambourg and played by a variety of pianists and instrumental combinations including military band well into the 1930s.

No doubt many fine pianists who were to reach maturity in the 1930s and 1940s winced when they recalled the trash they recorded in the 1920s. In 1927 Benno Moiseiwitsch recorded two flashy pieces by the unknown Chasins, 'Flirtations in a Chinese garden' and 'Rush hour in Hong Kong', and all did their stint on Beethoven's 'Moonlight' Sonata—all except de Pachmann who did not recommend himself to the record companies by saying, 'Beethoven's pianoforte sonatas are detestable. I used to play them all at one time, but I threw them over years ago.'

In 1927 the BBC agreed to take over the Promenade Concerts from private promoters, and the gramophone companies decided that they ought to do something to improve their image. The Columbia Gramophone Company jumped in with both feet and offered a prize of £2,000 for the best completion of Schubert's 'Unfinished' Symphony. The academics were aghast. Schubert had been happy to present it in its two-movement state in 1822, and had he wanted to complete it he had had six more years in which to do so.

Sir Walford Davies, a champion of music for the masses, up-held the scheme, and drew a tortuous analogy: 'Given a thousand casts of the Venus of Milo, what could be better for sculpture today than to set a thousand students (competitively, if need be) hunting for the perfect arms?' But Davies was in a minority, and the howls of protest were so loud that the rules of the contest were changed so as to require an original work conceived 'as an apotheosis of the lyrical genius of Schubert'. There was no surer way of bringing symphonic music into the common ken than by turning it into a kind of Bingo.

It was a world-wide movement, with juries of prominent musicians organised to choose local winners, and an international grand jury to meet in Vienna in 1928 to award the grand prize, which had been upped to $10,000. The prize was won by an obscure Swedish composer, Kurt Atterberg, for a medley of reminiscences. As Ernest Newman, the formidable music critic, wrote:

> Atterberg may have looked down the list of judges, and slyly made up his mind that he would put in a bit of something that would appeal to each of them in turn . . . if my theory is correct, the laugh is Atterberg's today.

Atterberg was evasive when asked if the symphony was a hoax, but Columbia took the opportunity to draw attention to the seventy Schubert recordings in its catalogue. It was an expensive lesson in public relations, and matters settled down once more, record companies realising that they were not in business for altruistic reasons. It was back to dance bands, operatic arias, military bands and novelty numbers. Dame Nellie Melba crawled back on to the recording platform for another juicy ballad. She was now sixty-three and it sounded like it.

CHAPTER SEVEN

THE CINEMA

IN 1908 THE SYNCHRONOSCOPE was unveiled at the Majestic Theatre in Evansville, Indiana. Its inventor prophesied: 'Talking pictures are the coming craze in all America.' But the Synchronoscope did no better than its predecessors, the patent taken out in 1880 to record sound by photography, Edison's Kinetophone of 1891, Demeny's Chronophotophone of 1982, or Oskar Messter's Chronophone. The latter was distinctive in that the sound was produced by compressed-air loudspeakers, and synchronisation was managed by using a special motor. A dial indicated the optimum picture speed to the operator. Most 'talkies' of the period simply tried to synchronise film and gramophone records; Léon Gaumont, the French film producer, recorded the sound on discs, and then filmed the action with appropriate gestures and lip movements to fit in with the sound.

The most promising work was done in the field of recording sound waves by photography, and in America Graham Bell, inventor of the first successful telephone, succeeded in transmitting (but not recording) sound by using light. The first man to take out a patent for the simultaneous recording of picture and sound on film was an English electrical engineer, Eugene Lauste, in 1906, using one half of the film for picture and the other for sound. There was no way to amplify the impulses, and after spending a fortune he gave up and allowed the patent to lapse.

Nevertheless he was on the right track. The principle was simple. A microphone is connected with an electric lamp which increases or decreases its light depending on the rhythm of impulses regulated by the sound reaching the microphone. The light fluctuations are recorded by a film band passing the lamp, and to transform these optical sound waves back into sound a positive print of the film is passed between a strong lamp with a thin beam of light and a photo-electric cell. According to whether the sound track is darker or brighter, the electrical resistance of the cell increases or decreases, and a circuit passing through it is modulated. The modulations are amplified and passed to a loudspeaker which transforms them into sound.

After World War I three German technicians began experimenting and shot a few trial films, but the German film industry was not interested, and the American film producer William Fox bought the rights for a few thousand dollars. The breakthrough was near. In 1920 Theodore Case patented his photo-electric cell system called Movietone. The thermionic valve, which made possible the electric amplification of recorded sound, was invented by the American radio pioneer Lee de Forest, and he followed this up with a novel incandescent lamp able to convert, with precision, current coming from the microphone into oscillations of light for the exposure of the film. In April 1923 Phonofilm was given a showing in New York, and picture-house owners were alarmed. Sound apparatus was expensive, and they were doing very nicely as it was. In England experiments with Phonofilm began in 1925 and the Empire Exhibition at Wembley in 1926 contained a booth showing talking pictures.

Warner Brothers took a step back in 1926 with sound-on-disc, but in 1927 went into the new system and made *The Jazz Singer*, starring Al Jolson. The talkie, for better or worse, had arrived, and those involved in the cinema business counted the cost. Among those hit the most were the musicians employed to play in cinemas, for the astonishing fact is that between three-quarters and four-fifths of *all* professional musicians made their livings playing in cinemas.

One of the most misleading misnomers is the term 'silent'

film, for it never was silent. In comparison with the riot of
sound that accompanied the pre-1928 film, talkies were restful.
In the heyday of the silent film there were 3,000 cinemas in Great
Britain, each in action for an average of fifty-nine hours a week.
The standard rates of pay were £2 per week for a 3–7 pianist, and
£3–£4 a week for an orchestral player working perhaps 3–10.30
with a two-hour break.

Although the cinema got into its stride only during World
War I, the implications had been seen before the war by far-
sighted managers. In 1913 the first cinema organ was installed in
the Palace, Accrington, the harbinger of all the rising monsters of
the inter-war years and after. Orchestras were not often used
before the war, and the task of accompanying the film was left to
a pianist, one of whom was interviewed:

> I play eight hours a day (40 minutes break at tea time) 2.30–10.30.
> I play in the dark and absolutely to the pictures. Of course, there
> are pianists who will simply strum a waltz or rag-time through and
> go on to the end of it, whether people in the pictures are dying or
> marrying. These are pianists not picture pianists. I knew of one
> girl the other day who, in a comic scene, actually played 'Onward
> Christian Soldiers'.

After World War I matters moved ahead rapidly, and in 1919
Novello published *Music for Small Orchestras Suitable for Cinemas*.
In 1922 Eugene Goossens conducted sixty-five members of the
London Symphony Orchestra to accompany the United Artists
spectacular *The Three Musketeers*. In the same year a writer in the
Musical Times declared: 'So long as a picture is absorbing, we
are hardly conscious of the music, though we miss it if it is absent.'
With a symphony orchestra conducted by a reputable man with
cue sheets and of sufficient status not to be bullied by the cinema
manager, no doubt an accompaniment to a film could be a
rewarding experience.

For most of the audience, any music was better than no music
at all. As a correspondent in the *Birmingham Post* put it: 'Where
there is no music within its walls the picture palace would be

for most of us a house of the dead, and we should be driven to any other form of entertainment that might chance to be heard.'

Orchestras varied enormously in size and quality, and personnel. The deputy system ran riot, and no player knew from one performance to the next who his neighbour might be. It could be a well-known experienced first violinist from one of the London orchestras willing to earn pin-money, or the rankest of amateurs who happened to be a drinking partner of the absent professional. For musicians who did not mind gigs and who could sight-read, the world of cinema music was undemanding, and there was a good deal of gentle amusement to be had in finding out what, exactly, was being played.

Eugene Goossens recalled:

> My happiest and most useful discovery was an August Enna, a prolific and soporific nineteenth century composer whose music provided an inexhaustible repertoire of tedious but appropriately varied symphonic accompaniment. It fitted everything, and also conveyed a spurious impression of great emotional depth, making it very suitable for my purpose.

Apparently Enna proved satisfactory, for Goossens was employed with the London Symphony Orchestra to do a film season at the Albert Hall in 1924.

Most of the audience did not realise what the orchestra was playing, but occasionally there is evidence that one or two most certainly did.

> In order to while away part of an afternoon I went to the cinema. The usual kind of sentimental film was being shown, and during a scene in which, if I remember rightly, some wealthy lady was falling in love with her chauffeur, I realised suddenly that the orchestra was playing music which was vaguely familiar. Imagine my horror when I knew it to be none other than the 'Et Incarnatus' from the B minor Mass! Needless to say it was being rushed through in a vulgar manner, but was nevertheless quite unmistakable.

S. W. Oliphant Chuckerbutty (where are you now, Mr

Chuckerbutty?), writing in the *Musical Times*, had a similar experience:

> I once heard a band attempting, of all things, Beethoven's 'Leonora' No. 3. The Introduction was started in brisk waltz time. The result, of course, was to arrive speedily at a complete standstill, and to evoke a priceless remark from the leader (who had never heard of the Overture until he bought it cheap from a commercial traveller) that it was not 'much cop', and that they would not do it again as it was 'duff'. At the next performance accordingly he substituted the 'Poet and Peasant', which they all knew. This conductor was drawing £15 a week, which is not at all a remarkable salary for a cinema conductor, but which is more than some accomplished cathedral organists make 'all in'.

The repertoires of the larger cinemas were large enough for the conductor or director of music not to be caught on the hop. The library of the Rialto contained 5,000 numbers divided systematically into categories:

Allegros	Minuets
Ballets & Dances	Misteriosos
Dramatic Melodies	Musical Comedies
Flowing	National Airs
Fox Trots	One Steps
Galops	Operatic Selections
Gavottes	Oriental Airs
Heavy Dramatic	Overtures
Indian Airs	Serious Melodies
Light Intermezzos	Songs
Light Opera Selections	Suites
Marches	Waltzes

For less ambitious cinemas there was Carr's *Cinemusic* of 1926, 'a series of loose-leaf books of music to suit all Screen Situations'. And there was the British Screen Music Society to advise on doubtful cases. In 1928 a guide came out for cinema conductors on Building Up Complex Emotions:

interior love	violin
exterior love	muted trumpet

study	French horn
comedy	trombone
idiot	bassoon
villain	double bass
suspense	drum

Orchestras were also used to play interludes between films, and some cinemas featured popular songs of the day. Louis Freeman, who controlled all the cinemas in Glasgow, declared to the *Melody Maker* in 1926 that 'there is no doubt but that the public at large likes this class of musical interlude just as much as the heavier classical compositions, which, beautiful as they are, may become irksome when one is fatigued from a hard day's work'. The works he had in mind were 'Babette', 'Sunny Havana', 'Save your sorrow' and 'Ukelele baby'. There was no mention of how he avoided the Performing Rights Society, then operating on behalf of 40,000 professional composers who had suffered a sharp decrease in their income owing to the lower sales of sheet music.

There were two schools of thought regarding the widespread

The Stoll opened in 1911 as an opera house, failed in 1913, and was turned into a cinema (Wonderful London)

use of classical music in cinemas. A minority thought that cinema orchestras brought good music to people who would not otherwise hear it, and that even jazzed up, distorted, or truncated in weird and wonderful ways it encouraged people to try to listen to classical music on the wireless or gramophone. Unquestionably regular cinemagoers associated certain pieces of music with certain situations, especially when they were accustomed to going to the local cinema where the conductor had worked out a formula, and it often happened that people who had no love for or inclination towards what they termed highbrow music could be moved by the performance of some popular classic that had been subconsciously associated with pleasurable emotion in the cinema. Consequently there are light orchestral works such as the overtures 'Zampa' or 'Poet and Peasant' that are as much part of the popular song heritage as 'Home, sweet home' or the 'Skye boat song'. More than anyone else, cinema musicians were responsible for the popularity of light orchestral music, broad-based music that demanded minimal attention and which, an extremely important point, hack musicians enjoyed performing.

There were others who thought that classical music in cinemas was disgraceful, others who admitted that a balance was difficult to find. To return to Mr Chuckerbutty:

> It must be borne in mind that the picture show is first and foremost an entertainment and not a concert. It is admittedly difficult to hold the balance between the various types of music, but at any rate one thing is obvious: whatever music is performed it should be played properly. Nobody who understands can possibly demand 'great' music all the time; it would be as bad to play the 'Siegfried Idyll' as an accompaniment to 'Felix the Cat' as it would be to play 'Felix kept on walking' for a Royal funeral procession.

With the immense popularity of the cinema, there was no shortage of money to employ what were advertised as full symphony orchestras. Although the unemployment figure in the mid-1920s was running at the 2 million mark this did not mean a diminishing attendance at the picture house—rather the reverse. Misery and fear were banished for a few hours, there was warmth

and comfort, there was music played by a live band—often the
only live music the poor heard—and there were plenty of films.
Hollywood was making 700 feature films a year.

As few of the audience knew what a full symphony orchestra
was, it was easy enough to make do with a combination that in
the larger houses consisted of three or four violins (no violas),
a cello, a double bass, a piano, a harmonium or organ, clarinet,
flute (no oboe), a cornet (no French horns), a trombone, and
drums, usually with attachments. Auditions were a farce, as the
managers or proprietors knew little about music. A conductor or,
in the big cinema, director of music could earn from £5 to £50
a week depending on his persuasiveness and charm. It was said
that the qualifications for being put in charge of a cinema orchestra were four in number:

1 Sufficient ability as a fiddler to stand up in the limelight three
times a day and play a fox-trot or waltz extremely slowly and two
octaves higher than written; together with an occasional essay
at what they call 'classical' music, ie 'Faust', 'Carmen' or the
Overture to 'Zampa'
2 A Semitic origin (but not name)
3 Preferably waved hair
4 A good waist for a dinner jacket

Almost everyone engaged in cinema work looked upon it as a
chore, to be endured with fortitude until, with a bit of luck, one
would end up as a musical director in a London prestige cinema.
In most cases it was a pose, for hours were reasonable, money
was fair and regular, and players were among others of their kind.
In addition, a musician need only be passably competent to get by,
and did not need the skills of a member of a genuine symphony
orchestra or the get-up-and-go of a dance-band musician. The
nearest parallel to be found today is in the member of the band of
a travelling circus troupe. Suddenly, the jobs were gone. The
only musician who could now find a firm berth in the cinema was
the organist, hired to play between performances and in inter-
vals.

The first talkie, *The Jazz Singer* of 1927, gave a clear indication of the future, and that the cinema would now make popular songs rather than use them. Composers perked up, with visions of huge sums to be made from royalties, performers were anxious, and cinema managers, worried about the capital expenditure of installing new equipment and wondering whether this was just a fad, were delighted by the enthusiastic public response. *The Jazz Singer* made 3 million dollars profit, and was followed by *The Singing Fool*. Al Jolson made memorable such ditties as 'Dirty hands, dirty face', 'Toot, toot, tootsie, goodbye', and, the tearjerker of them all, 'Mammy'.

The first true musical films arrived in 1929, Warner Brothers's *Gold Diggers of Broadway* and MGM's *Broadway Melody*, films that popularised 'Tiptoe through the tulips', 'Painting the clouds with sunshine', and 'Broadway melody'. The backlog of standards was raided for future essays in 'canned theatre', and relatively unknown composers were made rich by these unexpected bonuses, typical of these being Erno Rapee, whose 'Charmaine' (1926) was used in *What Price Glory?* and whose 'Diane' (1927) was used in *Seventh Heaven*.

These pioneering musical films were not received by some with the reverence that the producers thought they deserved, nor was everyman's hero, Al Jolson, who, in *Say It with Songs*,

> sings with provocation and without it, he sings even in the penitentiary, softening the hard mugs of crooks. No harm in that if the songs lilted or had fun; but they are all dreary, and all of the type in which the singer has to struggle to make the words fit the music; and since 'Sonny boy', in the same performer's *The Singing Fool*, was a winner, there is as its successor a paternal dirge of the same type called 'Little pal', not a single note of which, sung over and over again, are we spared.

So wrote E. V. Lucas, and Owen Seaman was no more complimentary about *Gold Diggers of Broadway*, which not only had talking and music, but was filmed in a kind of primitive colour. The programme assured its readers that it 'exceeds in pretentiousness [*sic*] and beauty anything which has yet appeared on the

Broadway Melody *was a pioneering singing picture, and the*
stage musical was never the same again

screen', and disclosed that the film related 'how modern gentle-
men are subtly bilked of cash and concomitants by these attractive
and clever metal gougers'. The production was roundly trounced;
what was the point of a 'dazzling beauty chorus of one hundred'
when 'their faces are about the size of a boot-button'? The singing of the key numbers was given to Nick Lucas, 'America's
crooning troubadour'. Owen Seaman liked him best 'when he
crooned like a tooth-comb without any words at all'. He also
took umbrage at the programme telling him that after each funny
scene there would be a lull so that the audience could recover in
time from its hysterics to follow the plot. 'When you see *The
Gold Diggers*', claimed the programme, 'notice how cleverly this
has been done.'

This feat of technique escaped Seaman ,who went on to compare
the clumsy and disconnected talkie with the old silent film, to
the latter's advantage. He summed up the situation thus:

> However, these fellows know their own business; and anyhow the
> perfected cinema will always retain certain peculiar virtues of its
> own; its cheapness, the limited length of its performances, the
> comfort of its spacious auditoria and the convenience of its veil of
> darkness.

Twenty million other British cinemagoers would have agreed
with every word.

CHAPTER EIGHT

THE COMING OF THE WIRELESS

THE FIRST WIRELESS shipping report was published by Lloyd's in 1910; by 1913 there were 30 shore stations and 435 naval vessels equipped with wireless; in 1910 successful tests were carried out in the United States over a distance of 490 miles, and during the war wireless technology progressed in leaps and bounds until by 1916 two-way communication was possible between aircraft and ground control, with an efficient screening apparatus that stopped interference from the aircraft engine. The historic message 'Hostilities will cease at 11 a.m.' was sent out from the Eiffel Tower on 11 November 1918, and was delivered to more than half the troops in France by wireless. The way was clear for the commercial and entertainment use of wireless.

The 23rd of February 1920 saw the opening of the first wireless telephone broadcasting service in the world, when a programme of vocal and instrumental music was transmitted for two half-hourly periods each day from Chelmsford on 2,800 metres. Amateurs and shipping companies were advised that this would take place and there were reports of good reception on crystal sets up to 1,200 miles and on valve sets up to 1,400 miles. On 29 April concerts were broadcast from The Hague, and in June and July other concerts took place at Chelmsford which in Europe were received by wireless and put through the telephone exchanges of large towns, and thence to subscribers' lines.

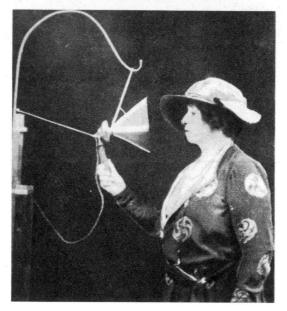

Dame Nellie Melba in full flow at an early microphone (Pageant of the Century)

The music encouraged a deal of unofficial listening-in, and in the United States manufacturers found an immense demand for receivers which they encouraged by setting up transmitting stations solely for the general public. The publicity brought enquiries from potential advertisers, and by 1921–2 the United States was enjoying a wireless boom, unlike Britain where advertising was frowned upon and private enterprise was distrusted. In June 1920, sponsored by the *Daily Mail*, Dame Nellie Melba had been persuaded to go in front of the microphone, and although initially unnerved by the 2,470ft mast (was she expected to climb up there?) she got through four songs including the ubiquitous 'Home, sweet home'. As it was a national occasion she also rendered the national anthem.

The Postmaster General put a stop to further tinkerings with the ether, but after considerable pressure had been put on the government the Marconi Company was allowed to put on one half-hour programme a week—Tuesday evening 8.00–8.30. Disasters did not fall thick and heavy after this concession, and a second station was permitted at Marconi House, London, with its call sign 2LO. By May 1922, 30,000 licences had been issued. In January 1923 a formal licence was issued to the British Broadcasting Company, and after a slow start broadcasting began in earnest.

The popular press resented the monopoly enjoyed by the British Broadcasting Company, and were scornful of the strict regimen imposed on listeners of news, weather, and concerts. The *Daily Express* declared that the monopoly was 'a cause of muddle and exasperation—poor programmes—listening-in licence a needless charge', and looked longingly at the United States free-for-all, where listeners got what they wanted not, as in Britain, what the BBC thought they ought to have.

The British Broadcasting Company (made a Corporation in 1927) was from the start run by strong men with nonconformist tendencies determined not to let the country collapse into a sea of drivel, and as there was no alternative the mass of the people accepted what they were given. They believed that the BBC was doing them a favour. Some indication of the appeal of wireless can be gauged from the sales figures of the *Radio Times* when it was first published in September 1923—a quarter of a million. At the end of 1925 there were 1,645,207 licensed listeners.

As early as January 1923 *The Magic Flute* had been broadcast from Covent Garden, despite the primitive equipment especially at the receiving end, and there were few concessions to popular taste. It may have been ambitious to broadcast Schubert's Unfinished Symphony with an orchestra of seven, but it seemed to prove that the BBC was bent on improvement and disdained to appeal to the lowest common denominator, as the less reputable gramophone companies were recklessly engaged in doing.

By the end of 1925 an average of 8,000 letters were sent to the BBC every week. In one typical week the critical ones were analysed (a mere 4 per cent of the total). One hundred and twenty-five condemned dance music, 65 were general grumbles, 52 were against alternative programmes (each station broadcast its own),

A wireless advertisement of *1923* (Ideal Home)

39 thought there were too many talks, 20 objected to individual artists, and one disliked religion.

In the early days the BBC welcomed letters, and even invited them from listeners. The man who might be termed the BBC's house musician, Percy Scholes, gave a talk entitled 'Is Bartok mad or are we?' and asked for listeners to send in their opinions. He received eight and a half sacks full of letters, and did not ask such pre-empted questions again. Private speakers were often deluged with mail, and one narrator of adventures cunningly encouraged people to write to him after each of his talks. Only afterwards was it realised that in each of the sessions the basic story was the search for a precious stone, and when his appreciative listeners thanked him for opening their horizons, he sent back a card explaining that he was the European representative of a New York jewellers, and at their service. He had successfully sidestepped the BBC's proscription on advertising.

Although record numbers were given, that was about the extent of the BBC's willingness to advertise. Dance-band conductors were not allowed to announce their own programmes, and household names such as Ford and Rolls-Royce were not permitted in scripts. The announcer had an instant cut-off if someone erred. The announcer was extremely important, and had to keep an eye open not only for surreptitious advertising but for impropriety, deliberate or otherwise. In 1928 the St George's Singers began their programme with three Elizabethan madrigals which, in sequence, made erotic reading: 'In going to my naked bed', 'Fair Phyllis I saw', 'To shorten winter's sadness'.

As the service moved from strength to strength stars were obliged to reconsider their attitudes towards it, some of them, including Sir Thomas Beecham, making themselves stupid in the process. In May 1924 Sir Harry Lauder said: 'I refuse to broadcast. If people want to hear Harry Lauder they must pay at the door.' A laconic account in February 1926 paints a different picture. 'Undoubtedly one of the greatest wireless successes of recent months has been the broadcasting of Sir Harry Lauder.' Beecham declared, 'If the wireless authorities are permitted to carry on their devilish work in ten years time the concert hall

ULTRA-MODERN RECEPTION

An ultra-modern advertisement for ultra-modern reception
(Ideal Home)

will be deserted.' One of Beecham's allies was William Boosey, the managing director of Chappell's, who in May 1923 wrote a letter to the *Daily Telegraph*:

> No one in the entertainment world is so foolish as to imagine that broadcasting can be opposed or wiped out. It has obviously come to stay. The objection of the entertainment world is against broadcasting under its present conditions. The first thing that the public should appreciate is that the Broadcasting Company is a big commercial concern exploited by very able business men . . .

The extraordinary thing was that the BBC was not exploited by 'very able business men'. It was aloof and disembodied, given an entity by Sir John Reith. It did not react to criticism, and when Chappell's found that it could no longer afford to run the Promenade Concerts the BBC took them over. Sir Henry Wood was not so disdainful as Beecham:

> Under the BBC the production of novelties is a pleasure, for the daily rehearsals have given me more time for new works . . . [the BBC] are able to tap all schools of music, from the classical to the latest brainwave in modernism and atonality, without the hindrance of the box-office brake.

In many ways the BBC did in its early days what Victorian music-hall proprietors were doing in the 1840s and 1850s— giving a captive audience a taste of quality. An entire new audience was being coaxed with good music. Listeners were not left to sort out the confusion for themselves, but were helped along by a number of excellent propagandists such as Percy Scholes (1877–1958) who had begun his educational work during World War I with his YMCA 'Music for the Troops', and Sir Walford Davies (1869–1941) who between 1926 and 1930 gave admirable talks on the wireless under the heading 'Music and the ordinary listener'. The BBC made classical music popular, and tried to make popular music classical. Only the best-behaved dance bands were allowed in the brief half-hour slots, and there was barely a hint of that quality which writers on jazz of the time called 'dirt'. One of these bands was Don Parker's Band, of the Piccadilly Hotel, which broadcast requests. It received 700 at a time, and the most popular tunes in 1926 were 'Babette', 'Sunny Havana', 'Araby' and 'Paddlin' Madelin' home'.

Other bands favoured by the BBC for late-night dance music included the Savoy Orpheans, the Savoy Havana, Jean Lassen's Band and Birt Firman's Band. There was little distinction between them via the medium of the primitive wireless set, though many felt that the Savoy bands got special attention and the Savoy was, in fact, an undercover branch of the BBC. Announcers certainly liked going down to the Savoy to announce the music played from there, for when they arrived just before

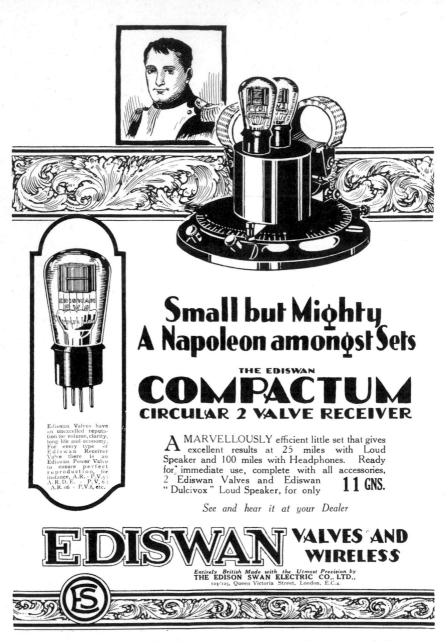

Small but Mighty
A Napoleon amongst Sets

THE EDISWAN
COMPACTUM
CIRCULAR 2 VALVE RECEIVER

A MARVELLOUSLY efficient little set that gives excellent results at 25 miles with Loud Speaker and 100 miles with Headphones. Ready for immediate use, complete with all accessories, 2 Ediswan Valves and Ediswan "Dulcivox" Loud Speaker, for only **11 GNS.**

See and hear it at your Dealer

Ediswan Valves have an unexcelled reputation for volume, clarity, long life and economy. For every type of Ediswan Receiver Valve there is an Ediswan Power Valve to ensure perfect reproduction, for instance, A.R. - P.V.5 : A.R.D.E. - P.V.6 : A.R. o6 - P.V.8, etc.

EDISWAN VALVES AND WIRELESS

Entirely British Made with the Utmost Precision by
THE EDISON SWAN ELECTRIC CO., LTD.,
123/125, Queen Victoria Street, London, E.C.4.

The text of this advertisement tells us something not revealed by the chronicles of the time—that the primitive earphones were more efficient than the much-vaunted loudspeakers (Ideal Home)

11 pm they knew that M. de Mornys, the Savoy entertainments manager, had laid on an excellent supper in a private room upstairs. Announcers, who were expected to be in evening dress at all times on account of the charisma of their profession, were able to let their hair down at the Savoy.

Save in their sampling of readers' mail, the BBC did not pay much attention to market research. Whatever the average listener wanted cut little ice with the programme-makers. Tastes were assumed to be low, and there did not seem much point in plumbing these unsavoury depths. However, the most enterprising of daily papers, the *Daily Mail*, ran a ballot and received a massive response, 1,285,083 votes. The musical preferences confirmed the worst fears of those who thought that if Britain followed the American pattern good music would be submerged under a sea of rubbish:

Variety and concert parties	238,489
Light orchestral	179,153
Military bands	164,613
Dance music	134,027
Symphony concerts	78,781
Solos, vocal and instrumental	72,658
Opera and oratorio	60,983
Glees, choruses, sea shanties	30,445
Chamber music	27,467

The wireless correspondent of the *Musical Times* found consolation in the high figures for light orchestral music, and pointed out the lowbrows' mistake in thinking that high-class music is represented only in symphony and chamber music concerts. Light did not necessarily mean trivial, and a light orchestral concert on 20 March 1927 consisted of music by Tchaikovsky, Saint-Saëns, Handel, Mozart, Mendelssohn, Elgar, Schumann, Debussy, and Chopin.

It is interesting to see that there was no category for popular music as such, and voters had to opt for dance music or variety and concert parties. Lovers of musical comedy and revue would be at a loss in determining where to put their crosses; these forms contained the bulk of the songs that are now looked upon as evergreens.

The remoteness of the BBC roused many listeners and composers to splenetic rage. Composers accused the BBC of shilly-shallying, and Albert W. Ketelbey, a popular composer of baubles such as 'In a Persian market' and 'In a monastery garden' (with monks chanting) became heavily sarcastic:

> As usual these artistic policemen who stand at the dangerous cross-roads of the broadcasting traffic and so kindly attempt to direct it to safety are rather illogical. On the one hand they infer that the general public is a common person of no nice discrimination while, on the other hand, they generally finished up with the sop that the public is the best judge.

The nearest the BBC came to explaining its position was in the answers to correspondents in its official organ, *Radio Times*. A listener who complained that there was too little dance music on the wireless was told: 'Our correspondent we are sure must appreciate that the BBC has to cater for a very large audience to many of whom dance music is distasteful.'

Many listeners believed that the BBC was cheating, that its desire to provide good music was phoney, and that it deliberately sabotaged musical relays by allowing (and encouraging) non-musical items to overrun their specified time. One writer to the *Musical Times* declared:

> I am perfectly ready to offer praise and thanks to the BBC for a great number of things. But the way they pander to the 'unmusical mob' and snub the musical minority fills me with annoyance. It is the most extraordinary thing, for instance, that it is almost invariably on the one, or at most, two evenings, in each week, when better-class music is being broadcast, that an extra talk or two is introduced. This was the case on two evenings running last week (and on numerous other occasions in the past). On last Wednesday the chamber music programme began late owing to an extra talk on the Eclipse, and on the next evening the start of the second portion of the symphony concert was delayed for nearly fifteen minutes owing to two talks, on 'Vimmen's Virk', by two German ladies.

Budding hopefuls for a wireless audition (Pageant of the Century)

The writer had a point. In one of his talks Sir Walford Davies set out to play the first movement of a Beethoven sonata. Halfway through he stopped and said, 'I'm sorry, but the tyranny of the time-table prevents me from finishing. I'll try to play it next week.' This was followed by five minutes silence, and then the continuation of a musical comedy that had begun earlier in the evening. A chamber work by Delius had been stopped in the middle of a movement (and on a discord!) to make way for the next item.

There were complaints, too, that certain transmission stations were privileged. An East Anglian listener deplored the fact that the BBC 'has begun one of those wretched periods when, to please the mob, Daventry is cut out of every symphony concert . . . while London will be continuing their symphony concert, Daventry is to relay selections from that dreadful type of entertainment called "Musical Comedy".'

From the heated controversy that surrounded wireless programmes one fact emerges clearly—musical taste was polarising, and the difference between highbrows and lowbrows was being exacerbated. The Victorians, anathema to all right-thinking 1920s people, would not have understood this. To them all music was acceptable, and a man could go from a symphony concert to a free-and-easy in a public house or a late-night music-hall performance and back for music in the home without any awareness that he was betraying his principles or, not to mince matters, his class. Broadcasting encouraged the belief that high-class people preferred high-class music; the presentation fostered this. Announcers were 'naice young men' who, it was sensed, deplored dance music and 'that dreadful type of entertainment called Musical Comedy'.

Rancour that had nothing to do with the music but only with the men and women listening to it began to intrude. Music that one did not like was intruding into the home, and this was regarded as a personal affront. When told that there was a simple remedy—switch off—the most amiable of folk had apoplexy. They paid ten shillings a year for the privilege of listening in, and although this was computed at a third of a penny (old style) a day (and there was broadcasting from 7 to 12), listeners were determined to get their pound of flesh, and if there was music that they hated then they would suffer it. It was a cross that had to be borne.

In non-musical items there was no kind of compromise, no pandering to popular taste. With the exceptions of dance-music programmes and certain humorous items, offerings were directed at an audience that would today be catered for by Radio Three and Radio Four. A debate between Basil Maine and Osbert Sitwell on the motion 'That opera is absurd' resulting in two half-hour orations would be tiring fare for even the most committed of Radio Three devotees. But this was a typical offering on a single-channel communication medium.

Although there were 2 million licence-holders by 1926 this still meant that there were more have-nots than haves. A close analogy can be drawn between mid-twenties radio and television in the early 1950s before ITV. A monopoly can afford to be smug and exclusive, especially when it knows that it is dealing with a predominantly middle-class consumer—for the cost of wireless sets remained prohibitive for the poor. The firm of Curtis advertised its range of wireless sets and wireless-gramophones (the term radiogram had not been thought of) with prices between £25 and £200. Burndept Ltd of the Strand offered

For your wireless

For your gramophone

Beautiful to look at

As an heirloom

THE WIRELESS TABLE

A handsome solid oak piece of furniture that houses your wireless and adds beauty to your home. 28 inches high. Twist legs. Cabinet for accumulators, etc. **£2. 7s. 6d.**
CARRIAGE & PACKING
3/6 EXTRA

PETER JONES LTD.
SLOANE SQUARE, S.W.1

The wireless table, a spin-off from the wireless and gramophone revolution (Ideal Home)

Mistress (pointing out cobweb). "HAVEN'T YOU SEEN THIS?"
New Help. "LOR, YES. SOMEFINK TO DO WITH YER WIRELESS, AIN'T IT?"

The wireless was a source of humour, often with a class bias
(Punch)

its basic two-valve Ethophone at £5 5s, but this was without valves, coils, batteries, or loudspeaker. Loudspeakers varied from £3 to as much as one wished to pay; the fashionable pleated diaphragm model was available at £7 7s. An adequate wireless set could cost one of the lower-paid workers up to a month's pay—at a time when the hire-purchase system was in its infancy. A member of the working classes could not envisage buying a motor car, could dream of a wireless set, but could afford a gramophone.

The wealthy who could afford a five-valve set were not so handicapped over the lack of choice, for in 1924 there were transmitting stations in London, Birmingham, Bournemouth, Cardiff, Manchester, Newcastle, Aberdeen, and Glasgow, all of them presenting different programmes. There was little networking. For the fortunate there was a wide range of fare—as one wireless set advertiser put it, 'News, talks on all manner of subjects, every kind of music from "highbrow" to jazz, stunt transmissions, and so on'. From the earliest days children were catered for with 'Children's Hour', with Uncle Arthur and Uncle Rex vying for kiddies' custom, and no issue of a woman's magazine was complete without a story of a child looking under a table or behind a chair, or in the set itself, for Uncles Arthur and Rex.

Punch ran a number of cartoons on wireless subjects, but true anecdotes requested by the *Radio Times* were difficult to cap. A Staffordshire collier was listening to the Savoy Havana Band in a pub with pleasure. 'Wind it up again, guv'nor,' he requested, 'let's have that one again!' A plebeian listener to the Savoy Orpheans thought that the applause that followed their performances denoted judicial pummelling. 'Leave the kids alone!' he called out, 'they were playing their best!'

The BBC and its programmes were seen through distorting spectacles. Sir Richard Terry trounced the BBC in a conference of the Industrial Welfare Society in Oxford:

> The music which comes over the wireless is for the most part on the same intellectual level as the old penny dreadful ... What would you say of an institution which gave out literature as the BBC gives out music, which gave you bits of Shakespeare now and then, but fed you for the most part on extracts from the penny dreadfuls. It is the populace which makes great music popular. It is the slack, middle-class people who prefer the worst—not the multitude!

Terry's attitude was shared by many, and the mezzo-brow was introduced into the vocabulary as a target for scorn. Musicians found the talks on musical appreciation by Sir Walford Davies patronising and unctuous, and the arrangements for military band of popular classics distressing and suitable only for humdrum minds; they considered that 'lower-class' music should be expunged from the wavelengths. Many of them suffered from the illusion that if the best were offered the average listener would disdain anything inferior. The *Daily Mail* poll should have settled that argument for all time, and in a Ripon rotary club address Dr C. H. Moody was wide of the mark when he declared: 'The vast majority will become musical when they have learnt the importance of the gulf between hearing music and listening to it.

The musical life of any country depends not so much on the work of the trained professional musicians as on the earnest, whole-hearted efforts of the people themselves.'

The hard line of the BBC was in keeping with the general mood of the Establishment in the 1920s. Its officials *knew* that they were right to dictate what the listener was to get. An autocracy did not permit working-class participation in popular music, and the power of the BBC as an extension of government meant that music made by and for the mass of the people did not get a look-in. Not until the monopoly of the BBC was cracked in the 1950s did home-made music (folk, skiffle, and rock 'n roll) make any nation-wide impact. The popular music broadcast in the 1920s was essentially middle-class and professional. When the BBC lifted up its skirts and announced a programme of jazz it was not the genuine article as played by Jelly Roll Morton or the black bands of Chicago or Kansas City, but the smooth counterfeit perpetrated by bland professionals in dinner jackets—what in the trade is known as Mickey Mouse music.

Those who complained of the middle-class domestication of music were not acquainted with American attempts to sweeten the classics or the efforts of British dance bands to kick the sacred cows up the rump:

> Hear Paul Whiteman, Hylton, and Debroy Somers render a popularised version of some classic. It may upset; then comes the realisation that it has an active, even comic verve, which is infinitely more virile than the monotone exactitude of a pedantic authentic rendition.

Whatever its faults (and in retrospect it seems clear that the BBC under Reith did a remarkably good job), few could have accused the Company and Corporation of that sort of sacrilege.

One of the most interesting observations on broadcasting came from H. G. Wells. Beginning with the customary chant that the BBC had not lived up to expectations and 'instead of first-rate came tenth-rate; the music was by the Little Winklebeach

Pier band', he went on to be remarkably and almost uniquely constructive:

> There could be one very fine use made of broadcasting, though I cannot imagine how it could be put upon a commercially paying footing. There are in the world a sad minority of lonely people, isolated people, endangered helpless people, sleepless people, suffering people who must lie on their backs, and who cannot handle books—and there are the blind. Convenient, portable, and not too noisy listening instruments now exist [1927], and for this band of exceptional folk I wish there could be a transmission, day and night of fine, lovely, and heartening music, beautiful chanting, and the reciting of a sort of heroic anthology . . .

Oh, wert thou living now, H.G.!

CHAPTER NINE

MUSIC FOR THE PEOPLE

WORLD WAR I had seen the end of the German bands, groups of excellent musicians who perambulated through the streets of town and city. The 1920s were less bothered by barrel-pianos, though there were still numbers of these instruments about. The absence of the German bands was more than made up for by large numbers of ex-servicemen who roamed the streets playing all manner of instruments. Many of these old soldiers had been wounded, and played instruments simply to avoid being booked by the police for begging. Those who could not play, wheeled gramophones through the streets on barrows or perambulators.

The immense popularity of the cinema brought queues, and these were catered for by buskers performing on every type of music-producing object. The buskers were at the bottom of the profession, for with the amount of work available in the 3,000 cinemas that existed up and down the country capable musicians had no difficulty in getting jobs, and with the seaside holiday an established habit there was good work available on piers and on the sands, in seaside concert parties and in pleasure gardens. Many excellent musicians played the season in places like Blackpool and Brighton in the hope that it would lead to better things; the Follies, the precursors of revue, had made the transition from pier pavilion to theatre, and there were many hopefuls waiting for their chance.

The brass band movement in the north of England kept going, despite poverty brought on by unemployment, wage cuts, and the fall in value of the pound. In times of recession industry was reluctant to spend money on buying instruments and uniforms for brass bandsmen in its employ, and because of the growing suspicion between capital and labour culminating in the General Strike of 1926 employers did not see why they should put themselves out to subsidise bands that would eventually play at the head of files of marching strikers. Gramophone records of brass bands were popular (though not so popular as military bands) and the better musicians from the north found recording sessions more agreeable than work in cotton mill and pit.

The peak of the brass band movement had been in the 1890s when there were reckoned to be 40,000 brass bands in the country, and as the twentieth century wore on numbers became less, despite the continuing popularity of contests, though the move to take contests to London from the recognised centre of brass competition, Belle Vue in Manchester, had not proved successful. The receding enthusiasm was partly due to new ways of passing time, and the cinema habit cut into practising time. Some of the enthusiasm of amateurs was dampened by the wide

The German band had disappeared from the London streets, but there were other itinerant musicians making up for them
(Wonderful London)

The decade was a paradise for buskers who worked
the cinema and theatre queues
(Wonderful London)

sale of brass band records; previously run-of-the-mill brass
bands had had little to compare themselves with except other
local bands of a similar standard, but when bandsmen heard the
virtuosos of their own instruments on record many realised that
they would never approach that standard of performance and
self-pride was damaged.

Surprisingly, oratorio kept going through the 1920s; one would
have thought that no form of music was more alien to the mores
of the time. In 1923 it was claimed that there was more musical
activity to the square mile in London than anywhere else in the
United Kingdom, and much of this revolved round amateur
choirs. This would have been impossible a quarter of a century

earlier, when the centres of choral singing were the north of England and Wales, but the factors that had damped down the brass band movement had also had their effect on the great choirs of Leeds and Huddersfield. There were more outlets for leisure time, and in those parts of the country hit hardest by the recession and where a high proportion of the 2 million unemployed were concentrated it is quite understandable that working people did not feel like singing.

Audiences were more critical of the northern sound—quantity not quality—and praise and deprecation were mingled when the Leeds choir came to London in 1925 to take part in Beethoven's Ninth Symphony: 'I don't know any choir that could sing so loudly, or that could so brilliantly meet the physical demands of the Ninth Symphony; but I know several in various parts of the country that could show more musicianship, alertness, and appeal.' The critic concluded his summary by saying that he could not 'avoid the conclusion that the prestige of Yorkshire singing has suffered a nasty jar'.

Favourites of choirs remained Handel's *Messiah* and Mendelssohn's *Elijah*, revamped by Sir Henry Wood and others to give big noisy choirs their head, but Elgar's *Dream of Gerontius* was showing amazing vitality. The modern English oratorio had been regarded as a one-shot work, to be performed at a Three Choirs Festival and then laid reverently to rest, but the enthusiasm of choirs and audiences for the *Dream of Gerontius* altered that. In the Festival of Britain in 1951 more choirs wanted to sing this work than any other, including *The Messiah*.

Many composers, envious of the popular success of the *Dream of Gerontius*, tried to emulate Elgar, and a good many oratorios were written during the 1920s, such as Walford Davies's *High Heaven's King* staged at the 1926 Worcester Festival and Granville Bantock's *Seven Burdens from Isaiah* performed at the 1928 Gloucester Festival, described by the editor of the *Musical Times* as a 'miscalculation with some splendid moments . . . a long stretch for an unaccompanied double choir sandwiched between elaborate fanfares for brass and drums'. The Three Choirs Festivals continued to offer a stamping-ground for such works, though these festivals were regarded by London-based musicians with amusement mixed with desperation. Sir Thomas Beecham had referred to the Three Choirs Festival with the contemptuous comment 'whatever they might be'.

It is interesting to see what choral societies were doing in the 1926–7 season. Certainly there is no doubt that oratorio was genuinely popular rather than fashionable. There were 62 performances of Handel oratorios, including 46 *Messiahs*. Elgar chalked up 38 performances, including 14 of the *Dream of Gerontius*. There were 20 *Elijahs*, and Coleridge Taylor's *Hiawatha* saga, that curious hybrid half-opera half-oratorio, continued to do well. Choral societies triumphed in concert versions of operas, such as Gounod's *Faust* and the Wagner operas, and the Edwardian light operas of Edward German, *Merrie England* and *Tom Jones*, received more attention from choral societies than from operatic companies. An odd popular choice was *The Mystic Trumpeter* by Hamilton Harty, a conductor best known for his arrangement of Handel's *Water Music*.

There were certain works that were rarely heard in the full panoply of a concert hall but were the staple diet of church choirs. Typical of these was Stainer's *The Crucifixion* (1887). Even Grove's *Dictionary of Music and Musicians* can find nothing more laudatory to say about Stainer than that he was reliable and efficient, and reserved praise for his organ-playing. *The Crucifixion* was ideally suited to enthusiastic but not very good groups of singers (a choir implies some degree of organisation).

Enthusiasm was most certainly the quality that marked the astonishing resurgence of community singing, a publicity stunt by the *Daily Express* that swept the country. Many believed that this was due to the vast crowds that congregated at football matches, and certainly the gramophone companies capitalised on this phenomenon, the Columbia company issuing (on number 4256, for present-day football followers of the club) a record of 14,000 lusty fellows on the Fulham football ground singing 'Land of hope and glory' and (on 9182) 'Who killed Cock Robin?', 'Loch Lomond', and 'O come, all ye faithful'. The singing on these records was slow to get under way, and was interspersed

Many believed that the community singing craze started at football matches. Wembley was opened in 1923, and the Cup Finals drew the singing talents of the nation (Pageant of the Century)

with catcalls, shouts, and the clatter of rattles, but there was none of the lese-majesty that marks the community singing of present-day football fans. A gramophone critic asked whether it was seemly 'to drag a great hymn into such a milieu'.

The craze was started off in 1926 when the *Daily Express* declared that 'for the last one hundred and fifty years the British people have had little or no opportunity of meeting in public to sing without restraint. The *Daily Express* will awaken the power of song once more in Great Britain'. Sir Henry Wood dismissed this as a 'burning though belated anxiety on behalf of popular choralism', while others were indignant that the *Express* was not aware that all over the country people were singing away like mad. Community singing, said C. Lee Williams, was traditional congregational singing writ large, and if he were twenty-five years younger 'nothing would give him greater pleasure than to follow up this promising movement . . . unison singing was the top, bottom, and middle of all community or congregational singing'.

*Selfridge's was the locale for one of the most stirring episodes
in the community singing saga* (Wonderful London)

The *Musical Opinion* slated the enthusiasm, and sent a reporter
to the Alhambra to see if Hannen Swaffer was correct when he
claimed that 'Community singing is performing a miracle.'
Swaffer wrote that if readers tried community singing at smoking
concerts or in their homes a new revival of the English spirit
would sweep across the country. The soloists engaged for the
Alhambra sing-in 'cut a sorry and ridiculous figure' in allowing
themselves to be 'dragged about in the cause of advertisement
and showmanship . . . Not even easy money to be picked up
could be regarded as sufficient justification for lending themselves
to a cheap-jack advertising stunt'. Other musicians felt more
sympathy for the soloists. As the *Musical Times* critic wrote:
'Imagine the kind of atmosphere set up by ten minutes' shouting
of "What shall we do with a drunken sailor?" and "Three blind
mice", and try to conceive the plight of the soloist who follows.'
Even non-musical journals joined in the furore. 'Let us be

under no illusion in regard to community singing', commented *The British Baker*. 'It is a jolly fine pastime, but it is no more an evidence of a renaissance of musical appreciation in England than a currant bun in a confectioner's window is an evidence that the confectioner is a first-rate wedding-cake decorator.' And, so far as the bread industry of Britain was concerned, that was that, but the *Express* reacted in shocked surprise to the attacks on its fine feelings, and hammered home proof of its good work in headlines:

COMMUNITY SONGS DRAW RECORD GATE
Community singing arranged by the *Daily Express* drew a gate of over 19,000 at Southampton yesterday in a football match between Southampton and Portsmouth.

An ironic commentator observed: 'We think it is likely that some came for the football as well! In fact, this particular match, on account of local rivalry, has filled the ground to "house-full" point for many years. Could there be a better instance of solemn, humourless "cheek" than the *Daily Express* claim?'

The national daily under Beaverbrook was on one of its emotional missions, and to further emphasise how the crusade was going amongst the *hoi polloi* it published an account of a sing-in amongst the employees of Selfridge's:

Thousands of pounds' worth of coloured silks and fineries formed a brilliant background to the 'set', and through the wide, deep well which cuts a vertical path from the roof to the ground floor, powerful electric lamps sent a shaft of golden light. The singing of these voluntary and enthusiastic 'supers' was extraordinarily beautiful. They revealed a true appreciation of time and rhythm. They also showed a fine sense of the stage, and took up effective positions amid the wax models and stands. Hundreds of others leaned over the balconies within the well, and harmonised with the singers below, while the lift girls, in their picturesque uniforms, stood at their posts and sang like a professional chorus.

It was a silly-season stunt that snowballed uncontrollably, but there were many who took the word of the *Express* as gospel, including Sir Richard Terry, who as an adjudicator heard much of the finest choral singing in the country. Hymn-writer, organist and director of music at Westminster Cathedral since 1901, and an authority on sixteenth-century music, he shared the cosmic view of community singing with the Beaverbrook press:

> People who come to community singing concerts are not concerned with merely singing notes, as are ordinary choirs. They respond to the feeling in the songs, and they are capable, as was the Colston Hall [Bristol] gathering tonight, of giving the truest value to emotions, colour, and pathos, out of sheer musical innocence.

Some took umbrage at community singing because, so far as they could see, the largest congregations were those at football matches. Gerald C. Forty addressed the Birmingham Rotary Club, and claimed 'there is more joy in heaven over a child practising scales than over fifty thousand community singers at a football match'. Lt-Colonel C. P. Hawkes saw community singing as opening the door for the revival of folk song, the 'genuine' popular music that for some reason the British public were reluctant to take to their bosoms:

> The English people were left with nothing to sing until, practically only a few months ago, the evangelists of community singing seized the opportunity with a nation ripe for the revival of folk-song proper.

Those who read this pricked up their ears. Could it be, after the long years of proselytising, that folk song, the *true* music of the people, was about to establish itself in the hearts and minds of the multitude? If it were, what a pity that the guiding spirit of the Folk Song Society, Cecil Sharp, had just died!

The folk-music revival, of which great hopes were entertained after the founding of the Folk Song Society in 1898, had not fully materialised, and although professional musicians involved in the movement were happy to use folk songs, suitably arranged and transfigured, the public at large did not understand what the fuss was about. Rural rituals were of no interest to a working class that was predominantly urban, and there was resentment when folk music was pushed because it was good for them.

Thanks to the endless endeavours of Cecil Sharp, folk music found its way into education. At the beginning of 1919 the historian H. A. L. Fisher, President of the Board of Education 1916–22, asked Sharp to call on him to discuss the best way of instilling into the minds of children 'a sense of rhythm and a love of our old English national songs and dances'. In 1923 Sharp was praised at the Imperial Education Conference as a man 'to whose work in this field British education owes an almost irredeemable debt of gratitude'. As an 'occasional' Inspector of Training Colleges, Sharp was tireless, though he had more than his share of irritations. At the Christmas Schools in London Sharp had to contend with incompetent administration and uninterested educationalists. Of one of these schools he wrote in December 1922:

> We open tomorrow with 578 students, 21 teachers, and 21 accompanists, a motor-bus service between the outlying rooms and the central building, and a rotten Director doubled up with lumbago, coughing and spluttering with bronchitis, and otherwise displaying symptoms of galloping senility.

Primary-school teachers were urged to include folk music in their curricula, and although many could not differentiate between a true folk song and an art song emulating a folk song it did not matter because, above all, folk music was healthy. The Victorian pioneers had cleaned up folk song, for, too often for its own good, folk song dealt with unashamed sex.

Reports of the activities of the Folk Song Society confirmed ill-defined suspicions that it was all an upper-class game played out in rarified surroundings, and when a meeting of the Musical Association at Central Hall, Westminster, in 1926 had as its lead speaker Arthur A. Pearson talking on European balladry a few sceptics went along to hear what he had to say. Pearson said that the traditional ballad had attracted the student of literature, the musician, the folklorist and the philologist, and had fascinated

*There was suspicion of the people involved in folk song
and dance, often justified*

'both simple peasants and men of high intellectual attainment'.
Someone should have told him that the word 'peasant' had
distasteful overtones to the man-in-the-street. Even the most
cultivated people who lived in the country were totally unaware
that 'a species of poetry and song was nurtured by farm labourers
and old women in a sort of secrecy that was amazing'.

At various points in his lecture Mr Pearson came out with
various folk songs from all the nations, and in a discussion after
the talk Dr J. C. Bridge uttered a warning against decrying the
Middle Ages, and doubted whether there was as much ignorance
as people supposed. He found it remarkable that the main bulk
of folk-song ballads should have lain between the borderland of
England and Scotland. So, no doubt, did many of the Folk Song
Society who had done field work in the west country, Sussex and
Suffolk, and when Bridge offered the theory that the border
country work was done by one great poet there were sound

grounds for dismissing him as a crank, the kind of person the society could do well without but who was attracted to it like a burr to a trouser leg.

If, to most people, folk song was puzzling, folk dancing was risible, and enthusiasts paid too much attention to the success of folk dancing when it was introduced into the Army in 1917 under the auspices of the YMCA. It became popular at convalescent depots, and twelve members of the English Folk-Dance Society were busy in France teaching soldiers the rudiments of the Northumbrian Sword Dance, favoured because, it was said, 'a man likes the feel of a tool in his hand'.

Only a handful of the soldiers who had danced in France joined the society, and although the King's Theatre, Hammersmith, was taken for a week in 1921 and folk dancing performances were given every evening plus two matinees to critical acclaim ('open-air sweetness . . . cleanness . . . wholesomeness') folk dancers seeking to re-awaken the old rituals with Morris dance and the like were often, if *in situ*, pelted by the local children.

Ralph Vaughan Williams had been a leading light in the Folk Song Society, and spent a lot of time on its behalf (Lambert)

*Community singing had been practised by the army, though
without the publicity of the later development*

In 1927 the All-England Festival of the English Folk-Dance
Society opened at the Albert Hall, inefficiently stage-managed
as is the unfortunate lot of well-meaning movements. 'Everything
points to the possibility that in ten or twenty years time the
country dance will again be truly national' wrote an enthusiastic
observer, watching groups from a dozen countries. A troupe
from the Appalachian Mountains was considered a spectacle
that Diaghilev should have seen, and the North Skelton sword
dancers acquitted themselves well in the Morris dance. A team
of elderly gents in their sixties shuffled round in a Durham sword
dance, and a touch of the exotic was lent by a jocund but un-
animated twelve-strong group from Holland.

The festival was rounded off by Vaughan Williams, who
conducted the dance band, encouraging the assembly in song,
'in which the assembled thousands made but a puling sound.
Not one in twenty seemed to know the tunes, and all seemed
afraid of their own voices. The children of today know more
about English folk-songs than do their elders.' How different from
community singers who, although not one in twenty among them,
too, seemed to know the tunes, were certainly not afraid of their
own voices or concerned with academic propriety.

When there was no supervision tunes were served up—including the folk songs that the purists liked so much—with obscene and doubtful lyrics, in many cases restoring a quality that the tunes had once had but had lost in emasculation. Community singers took a lead from soldiers in World War I, who freely amended tunes, including those from musical comedy such as 'They didn't believe me' which with its new words was an ironic damning indictment of the war game.

The songs that were sung spread right across the whole field of music—folk songs, pseudo-folk songs, sea shanties, hymns, drinking songs, ragtime ditties, musical comedy songs, and music-hall songs. All were strained through the same sieve, and came out bellowing parodies; but unquestionably this was genuine popular song, and gave a truer indication of what the masses thought was worth-while singing than any other fount of knowledge.

Among them were pieces difficult to classify, such as the song 'Abdul' the Bulbul Ameer', believed to have been composed by William Percy French for a college smoking concert at Trinity College, Dublin, in 1876, and first published in London ten years later. Perhaps the most famous of community songs is 'Abide with me', written by the Reverend H. F. Lyte about 1847 and put to music by William Henry Monk (1823–89), a little-known composer who studied music under a number of nonentities, and was organist at several chapels, being appointed director of the choir at King's College, London, in 1847. In 1874 he became a professor of vocal music, and was one of the musical editors of *Hymns Ancient and Modern*, in the 1861 edition of which 'Abide with me' appeared under the title 'Evening'.

'O come all ye faithful', sung because it was well known (often the sole criterion for community singing), is a translation of 'Adeste Fideles', probably composed and written by John Francis Wade about 1750. Frederick Oakeley (1802–80) gave choirs the familiar words in 1852. 'After the ball' was a song that was sung in drawing-room, saloon bar, and elsewhere, composed by Charles K. Harris, an American banjo-player and lyricist, in 1892. It was sufficiently in the folk repertory for

The Vesper Hymn.
(Abide with me.)

"The shades of evening fall, the bells are pealing,
  A message sweet of peace from heaven above;
While in the church a fragile form is kneeling,
  Whose aching heart seeks sympathy from above.
Unknown, uncared for in the wide, wide city,
  Upon her pathway shines no ray of light,
An orphan, weary of the world's cold pity,
  She prays that heaven will guide her feet aright:
'Abide with me! fast falls the eventide;
  The darkness deepens; Lord, with me abide.'"

'Abide with me', the community singers'
anthem

Jerome Kern to use snatches of it in his musical *Show Boat*
of 1927.

'All through the night' is anonymous, printed in 1784 with
Welsh words and an English translation, and announced as
being 'preserved by tradition and authentic manuscripts from
remote antiquity'. 'Alouette' was a French-Canadian song, first
printed in 1879, and although chiefly found in the school-room,
where it formed a useful link between French and music lessons,
it was sung on more genteel occasions orientated to Boy Scouts'

sing-songs and the like. 'Annie Laurie' was based on a romance
between members of two rival Scottish clans about 1705, and
the words were first printed in 1823. It is a first-class example of
the phoney folk song, the music being composed by Lady John
Scott in 1835 and published in *Vocal Melodies of Scotland* (1838),
apparently without her consent.

'Auld lang syne' is probably the highest scorer of all time; the
words 'Should auld acquaintance be forgot' were established by
James Watson in 1711, and the tune is authentic folk, traced
back to at least 1687, and called 'I fee'd [see'd?] a man at
Martinmas' before being united with the ubiquitous words in
1798. 'The band played on' ('Casey would waltz with a straw-
berry blonde . . .') was not a typical community song, but it had
the right lilt and simple melody for it to be used. The music was
composed by the obscure John F. Palmer, and the song was
first published in an 1895 newspaper.

'Barnacle Bill the sailor' arrived at the fag-end of the
community-singing craze, but was very suitable for bawdy,

*Some community songs were filched from the Boy Scouts, a very
popular movement in the 1920s* (Pageant of the Century)

'Bollocky Bill' being its public-bar cognomen. 'Beautiful dreamer' was a Stephen Foster number of 1864 (his last song), and 'The bells of St Mary's' (simple words, simple music, thus popular amongst singing mobs) was an ordinary shop ballad composed by A. Emmett Adams (1890–1938) with words by Douglas Furber, a musical-comedy writer. It was published in 1917.

'Blow the man down' was a typical gusty sea shanty, claimed by the Americans to be theirs and dated 1879, but probably earlier, and certainly not a corruption of a Negro song 'Knock a man down' as was also claimed. 'The British Grenadiers' was discovered by Victorian musicologists to date from the mid-eighteenth century, and the tune has been variously ascribed to Dutch, English, Scottish, and Irish sources. Rather too rapid for an average community sing-song, it was a semi-trained choir piece, as was 'The Campbells are coming', claimed as originally a country dance called 'Hob and nob' and authentically old, first put into print about 1745. 'The Camptown Races' was an 1850 Stephen Foster song, and is supposed to have triggered off the sea shanties 'Doodah' and 'Hoodah'.

American minstrelsy did well among the community singers, a typical example being 'Carry me back to old Virginny' (1878), music and words by James A. Bland (1854–1911), a pioneer Negro songwriter, but this was a minority piece compared with 'Clementine'. The words of this popular favourite were set down in 1863, the music in 1884, with Percy Montrose credited, and although references to 'forty-niner' and 'canyon' imply an American origin, American experts speculate that it may have been an English song.

'Colonel Bogey', by the prolific band composer Kenneth J. Alford (alias Frederick J. Ricketts), was wide open for lewd words when it was first published in 1914, but it was more often heard as a marching song than for a stand-up-and-sing. 'Come back to Erin', popularly supposed to be a folk song, was an ordinary royalty ballad of 1866 by Claribel, real name Charlotte Alington Barnard (1830–69), who submerged the mid-Victorians under a flood of rubbish, though she was not, as here, often let loose on the music as well as the lyrics. Another pretended folk song was 'Come to the fair' (1917), music by Easthope Martin (1882–1925), a rousing ditty eminently suited to being bashed out by massed voices. 'Comin' through the rye' was originally a bawdy off-shot of 'Auld lang syne' and a Burns version was posthumously published about 1800. The alternative opening line, 'Gin a body' for 'If a body' is not obscene—they mean the same.

A quintessential bar-room favourite was 'Down by the old mill stream', a mawkish 1910 American ballad by Tell Taylor. 'Drink to me only with thine eyes' was published in its present form about 1780, and some say that Mozart wrote the music, though most do not. It started off life as a glee. The tune of 'What shall we do with a drunken sailor' dates back to 1824, and throughout the century was served up with various words and in major and minor keys, the British preferring the minor and the shanty.

'For he's a jolly good fellow' is a group song rather than a community song, and if it is heard the chances are that someone is getting the sack and/or a gold watch, politicians are lurking, or there is a good deal of drink about. It made its initial appearance in France in the eighteenth century, was anglicised and boozified in the 1840s, and was published as an English folk song in 1905, with learned speculation that it was an old hunting song.

'Home, sweet home' is the type of community song found on records, but not the kind of thing a crowd would sing spontaneously. It is a number from Henry Bishop's 1823 opera *Clari, or the Maid of Milan*, and no self-respecting singer could miss it from her repertoire. 'I wonder who's kissing her now' was not a football crowd singing-piece, but was very popular (and still is) at working-class weddings, having the dreary lilt and predictability that suit the milieu. It was a typical American pot-boiler of 1909, as was 'Ida, sweet as apple cider' (1903).

'I'll take you home again, Kathleen' is often mistaken for an old Irish ballad instead of an American popular song of 1876, words and music by Thomas P. Westerdorf, and there is also ambiguity about the 1877 'In the gloaming', by Lady Arthur Hill, otherwise Annie Fortescue Harrison. 'It ain't gonna rain no mo' ' was claimed to have been a modern (1923) version of a southern melody, words and music by Wendell W. Hall, and because it was relentlessly plugged by the gramophone companies in time for the community-singing boom it was incorporated into the canon.

One of the wartime songs that continued to haunt the community singers was 'It's a long, long way to Tipperary', promoted by Marie Lloyd in 1912 and turning out to be one of the best of all marching songs. 'I dream of Jeanie with the light brown hair' was another Stephen Foster number, this time of 1854. 'Jingle bells' was strictly a seasonal number, but was suited to community singing. Written by James Pierpont in 1857 for a Sunday-school entertainment, it rapidly established itself as Christmas incarnate.

'Let me call you sweetheart', composed by Leo Friedman in 1910, was for bar-room sing-songs, but 'Little Annie Rooney' was more versatile, an 1889 music-hall song by Michael Nolan, an Irishman who worked the halls. 'Little brown jug' was an 1869 American song by Joseph Winner. 'Loch Lomond' was made popular by stalwarts of the halls such as Harry Lauder and Will Fyffe, and there is a good deal of dispute about its origins and whether it is a pseudo-folk song of 1845 or if it does, indeed, deal with the departure of Bonnie Prince Charlie to Scotland, in which the 'low road' is the grave.

At one time it was a favourite hobby to fit words to the 'Londonderry Air', but Fred E. Weatherly was the winner with 'Danny Boy'. 'Just a song at twilight', the boozer's lullaby, was written by J. M. Molloy in 1884. Like Weatherly, Molloy (1837–1909) was a barrister. 'Mademoiselle from Armentières' was another left-over from the war, a nostalgic 'must' for gatherings of old soldiers. 'Mary's a grand old name' was composed by George M. Cohan in 1905, 'Mighty lak' a rose' (1901) was by Ethelbert Nevin, but these were marginal pieces compared with 'Men of Harlech' and 'The minstrel boy', a favourite of record companies and of undoubted age, certainly earlier than 1813 when it was first put down in black and white.

'Mother Machree' ('Sure I love the dear silver that shines in your hair') was a bit of American blarney from 1910 (music

Chauncey Olcott and Ernest R. Ball), taken over by community singers from the golden-voiced John McCormack, and with 'Nellie Dean' we have the apotheosis of boozy togetherness. 'My bonnie lies over the ocean' first saw light in a volume of American students' songs in 1881, without credits and no doubt considerably older. Slave songs from America, many of them first published in 1867, were sung by semi-amateur choirs indoors but not often by the bellowing tyros, and this was true of the wide range that came under the heading of 'coon songs' such as 'Oh, dem golden slippers' by the composer of 'Carry me back to old Virginny'.

Of all the composers who supplied work suitable for the community singing perhaps Stephen Foster provided the most. In addition to those mentioned earlier there were 'Poor old Joe' (1860) and 'The old folks at home' (1851). Their treatment in England was not as adventurous as in America, with its tradition of four-part harmonising in barber-shop quartets. The accent in Britain was on unison singing, which paralleled the trend in northern choir singing—sheer sound without subtlety. Barber-shop quartets could make something from ordinary songs such as 'Sweet Genevieve' (1869) that were stretched on the rack by the community singers. No doubt many folk-song lovers, when they heard what the masses were doing to simple, agreeable tunes, wondered whether the common folk singing their heritage constituted a movement best smothered.

Tin Pan Alley, ever ready to jump on to some passing vogue, was caught on the hop by community singing, though Novello put through an enlarged edition of *The Pocket Sing-Song Book* (price 1s 6d), but by the time the Denmark Street publishers issued their sheets of community songs the nation had sunk back into lethargy, afflicted by laryngitis and a surfeit of jolliness. The tunes were ceded back to their customary copyholders— amateur and church choirs, the Boy Scouts, schoolchildren at their music lessons, and the reeling patrons of the public bar. They still sang at football grounds but it was no longer a phenomenon that would wrench Britain up by its shoelaces into a new and brighter life.

CHAPTER TEN

THE POPULARISERS

SUPPLY AND DEMAND was the law of Tin Pan Alley, and some of its ethics seeped into other musical fields including symphonic music. The hard sell was applied to Beethoven as well as Horatio Nicholls, mainly to popularise classical gramophone records but also to persuade the uncommitted that the wealth of good music transmitted on the radio was worth listening to. There was also the wish to get musical directors of cinemas to adventure further than 'Poet and Peasant'. What the cinema trade called high-class music was amenable to roughing up by bored, languid musicians in the orchestra pit.

It is not difficult to popularise something like Beethoven's Fifth Symphony, but it is difficult when the music is basically unpopular and the promoters insist that it be played using the original instruments—which is what revivalism often is. But not always; there was some revivalism in the 1920s that was concerned with stripping away Victorian excrescences, in stream-lining a music form for a modern age by going back to essentials. In religious music, hymns were updated in *Songs of Praise* in 1925, with Vaughan Williams involved with the tunes, though the revivalist hymn was never to receive the publicity it had in 1905 when two American evangelists conducted eighty-five daily consecutive meetings with attendances at each of 10,000 worshippers. Attempts were being made to reinterest Christians in plainsong, and Plainsingers and Anglichanters continued to indulge in internecine warface. The Edwardians had given carols a face-lift, and these had found a place in the Christmas repertoire.

The leading figure in the revival of old instrument music was Arnold Dolmetsch (1858 1940), who tended to agree with the folk-music enthusiasts that if old forms were brought back the masses would eschew modern counterfeits. The Dolmetsch family was the do-it-yourself family extraordinary; they made their own instruments, they reasoned out a work's original format, they selected a repertoire of which no one else had ever heard, and they performed and danced their discoveries. The Haslemere Festival of Ancient Chamber Music had apparently been going on for ever, and old Arnold had outlived almost everybody who had thought him barmy—all except Bernard Shaw, who was as contemptuous of harpsichords and clavichords (likening them to jangling bell-pulls) as Dolmetsch was of the modern pianoforte.

If Dolmetsch had been a magician, Percy Scholes wrote, he would have 'waved a vigorous wand and transformed all the world's iron-clad pianofortes overnight into gentle wooden harpsichords and clavichords, feeling that in doing this he was carrying out a great and much-needed work of moral purification'. He wandered with his family into the 1920s like a character from an Arthur Rackham drawing. Arnold Bennett had seen him in 1926; he was 'just like a gnome, hair all over his face, and a strange, clear, pure, impish, masterful glance'. Just as contemporaries had described Dolmetsch forty years before.

The Dolmetsch milieu was the William Morris arts and crafts movement translated to another age, and both were handicapped by the fact that the modern methods were more convenient. Dolmetsch had been giving concerts since 1889, and the standard of performance rarely approached virtuosity or even competence; the medium really was the message. The Haslemere Festival attracted strange audiences to hear antique music by unknowns played on viols and gambas. A typical number from the 1927 festival was a sixteenth-century saltarello 'danced with much grace, with castanets, by Mrs. Dolmetsch, to a very pretty

Italian tune played on the lute only by Mr. Dolmetsch'. On the lute only, and extremely faithful, no doubt. If there was a demand for a particular composer Dolmetsch was suspicious. 'We play neither Byrd nor Gibbons', he announced coldly, 'we do not like them. We play nothing that is the accepted fashion.'

Yet despite this kind of reverse selling Dolmetsch was responsible for reviving an instrument that has become a school band 'must'—the recorder, which he reconstructed in 1926 after two centuries. By 1930 he had a consort of five, with Carl Dolmetsch the leading performer. The lute was more of a problem, for Dolmetsch had to find out for himself the technique as well as the construction, problems he overcame in 1929. There was no record of the rebec playing art music, so when he had made one Dolmetsch had to scrabble around for suitable material. And there were the serpent, the shawm, the dancing-master's fiddle, pipe and tabor, and the lyra da braccio; once Dolmetsch was discovered playing a hurdy-gurdy.

Unquestionably Arnold Dolmetsch was a character, and in 1928 a number of sympathisers including Vaughan Williams and the Poet Laureate, Robert Bridges, formed a Dolmetsch Foundation to carry on the good work, one of the consequences being the house magazine *The Consort*. With the death of Arnold enthusiasm for sixteenth-century music diminished, but after World War II there came an upsurge of interest, capitalised on by the record companies when the long-playing record had gobbled up all the standards. Dolmetsch certainly lives.

Cults are by their definition esoteric. To many, Dolmetsch was more interesting than the music he and his family were playing, and it is very clear that promoters thought the same about a few of their high-class properties. The gramophone companies built up the images of their opera stars, and even adverse publicity. brought in audiences to hear Beecham and de Pachmann, if only to find out what outrageous thing they would say next. Beecham was a never-ending fount of impudence. In an interview with a *Derby Daily Express* reporter after a Nottingham concert he said that the town was no better than a zoo, and the audience 'look as if they have been feeding in grass for the last three years, like the king in the Bible'. Very amusing, if one did not live in Nottingham.

And the choleric colonel class was tuned in to Beecham's comments on the media that gave him his bread and butter: 'If people cannot get decent musical food, that is no reason why you should give them poison. Rather than wireless or a gramophone, take prussic acid at once.'

Classical music was made palatable by coating it in sugar icing, by reading extra-musical significance into individual works, and by romanticising the lives of the composers; there was but a thin line between the efforts of the musical appreciation instructors on the radio and the promoters who liked to package Strauss (Richard) like Straus (Oscar). They would have liked good music to be a sequence of Beecham-style lollipops, rather than pretty tunes embedded in a record-time-consuming parcel labelled symphony or concerto.

Efforts to cope with the incomprehensible or brighten up what editors privately thought were boring topics do not need a commentary:

Handel's 'Messiah' was given in the Cathedral today . . . This beautiful oratorio was nicely presented. (Hereford paper)

It was Chopin who gave to the world the soul of the night. He was a comet that passed across the face of the musical sky to blaze a way to glory. His name is pronounced *Show-pang.* (weekly paper)

Bach was the most human of all composers . . . His name is pronounced Bark. (weekly paper)

Climax after climax he built up, his recaptured baton strangely like a rapier playing against a hundred adversaries; his left hand calling for more bass, more drums, more everything; until, with a last encircling sweep of his baton, he brought the march to a crashing finish and brought the audience to their feet. (*Daily Express* on a 1927 Beecham concert at the Albert Hall)

Had Beethoven [1770–1827] in the Ninth Symphony and Mass in D more closely followed Handel's or Mendelssohn's [1809–1847] treatment of the voices, the effect would have been even greater. (*Irish Independent*)

One music correspondent of a provincial paper summed up all the desperation of the person who has no idea what is going on, and is searching for an angle. He (or she) was appointed to go to a piano recital, where the lady pianist 'endeared herself to the audience' by leading off with a Prelude and Fugue from 'The Well-Tempered Chavichord[*sic*]', following up with some Brahms, 'doing this never-to-be-forgotten musician every justice'. The account of a Scriabin piece was mumbo-jumbo of the most mind-boggling kind: the 'breadth of harmonic [*sic*] outline in "Pathetic" by Scriatine [*sic*] was truly sustained throughout the performance'. The plum of the critique was:

> . . . and Miss ——'s triumph was undoubtedly secured by her effort at Liszt's 'Mazeppa', which described in music the shrill shrieks of a maddened steed to whom has been strapped a blood-bedraggled horse-stealer, named Mazeppa, who becomes free from the horse, this passage being portrayed by an ominous quietness which culminated in a grand finale as the freed horse dashes off to its herd.

The musings of bog-headed provincial journalists are of not much intrinsic interest except as comic relief, but they do illustrate the *wish* to enter the new musical world opened up by mass exposure of great music of the past through the wireless and gramophone. If Beethoven or Brahms were not popular, it was certainly not the fault of newspaper writers trying to put them over in the language of a twopenny novelette. There was a wealth of kindly feeling towards what journalists thought of as high-class music.

In one way this was a spin-off from a kind of greed. Listeners to the wireless wanted their money's worth, and if a Beethoven symphony was taking up half an evening, by God, they were going to sit through it. It was possible to make grand music matey by bringing it down to the level of the common deno-minator, drawing analogies with the music played for silent films, and demonstrating that it could be an integral part of life, accentuating the hearing of music rather than the listening to.

A feeling of togetherness and the sharing in masterworks

was obtained by asking famous men and women their feelings about music, or what were their favourite tunes. There were some surprises, and the project was ruthlessly cut down to size by the arch-enemy of pretension and gimmick, Bernard Shaw: 'Only people in a deplorably elementary stage of musical culture have favourite tunes. The question is a monstrous insult.' The composer Lord Berners was as arch and po-faced as his music. 'My favourite song is "The last rose of summer" . . . If by "singer" you mean any kind of singer, then the one I prefer is Little Tich. But, on the other hand, if you mean merely concert singers, please substitute Clara Butt.' The novelist W. J. Locke, God's gift to lending libraries, replied, 'My favourite song? I have heard thousands of beautiful songs . . . Dame Clara Butt, in my own house on New Year's Eve a year or so ago, sang "The Swanee river", and made me weep like a cow.'

It was readily assumed that top people liked top music, and the flippancy of some choices was shocking, rather like hearing a vicar swear. In 1920 the literary weekly *John o' London's* asked a number of eminent writers and artists whether they liked music. Joseph Conrad loved music 'without knowledge but with a great and profound emotion'. Mrs G. K. Chesterton wrote to say: 'My husband just asks me to inform you that he is so ignorant of music he does not even mind it.' Rose Macaulay wrote: 'I have never learned anything about music, and certainly am not musical; but I like to hear it, particularly bad music. I know when it is bad, but still enjoy it. I don't mind good either, if the other is unobtainable.' John Masefield, the poet, said simply that he loved music. H. G. Wells wrote: 'I like classical and some modern music very much—but not to the extent of going to the opera. Music has to come to me and I don't want more than an hour of it at a time. Subject to these limitations it delights and pleases and refreshes me.' The novelist John Galsworthy thought the question an insult to a civilised man:

Affected by music? I should just think so! By nothing more. My creative muse feels like a garden—or shall we say a weed-bed?— in a drought when it gets no rain or dew falls of music. But music is for me like poetry: I like or dislike very definitely, with physical sensations of delight or of irritation. I'm not at all catholic, and not at all learned. I know not in the least why I can't bear Wagner and love the 'Songs of the Hebrides', Gluck's 'Orpheo', Cesar Franck's Violin Sonata, or Ravel's Pavane; why I dislike Meyerbeer and love 'Carmen', or why the same I should listen with rapture to Chopin and the Matthew Passion.

The naturalist W. H. Hudson declaimed, 'I like music; so does everybody—except those who don't like it. But these are an insignificant minority and do not count.' Mrs Belloc Lowndes, a novelist best known for a book based on Jack the Ripper, liked eighteenth-century music, and preferred hearing music adequately if not superbly performed at a friend's house rather than go to the trouble of attending concerts. Sir Arthur Conan Doyle said that most music annoyed him, especially in restaurants and 'other inappropriate places'. He felt that there was music that would move him greatly, but had never got round to finding it. The author of country novels, Eden Phillpotts, disclosed that music was not essential to his happiness, and although he liked orchestral music he would not go out of his way to hear it. W. W. Jacobs liked military bands, piano-organs (he probably meant street pianos or barrel-organs), and bagpipes. He could take sad and solemn classical music neat, but otherwise he needed an easy chair, a bright fire, and a cigar to cope with the demand on his faculties.

The artist John Collier, a producer of meticulous conversation and historical pieces for the Royal Academy, was the know-all Philistine at his most unctuous. He was a passionate lover of music—if it did not distract him from 'more important occupations such as eating my dinner'; music lasted too long— musicians never knew when to stop. It had the disadvantage 'that one tune so closely resembles another that I never can tell them apart. Surely there must be something wrong with an art which shows such little variety?' Worst of all, music was entirely divorced from the intellect, made no appeal to the mind but only to the emotions (which was immoral). The novelist Hugh Walpole thought that music, literature, and painting were so closely allied that he could not imagine a practitioner in one of the arts not appreciating the others. The popular novelist Gilbert Cannan used the poll for a display of one-upmanship; he preferred silence to music, but César Franck and Stravinsky had influenced him more than any other modern artists. (Modern artists? Franck had been dead for thirty years.)

A caustic rejoinder by Ernest Newman to these confessions was as pointed then as it would be now.

> For most of them music is evidently a more or less agreeable form of ear-massage or nerve-massage, the pleasure it gives them being on about the same intellectual level as face-massage at the hairdresser's . . . this is our literary intelligentsia!

The 1920s was the first age of background music, the first when music could be aural wallpaper. For a growing portion of the public, the term 'pleasant sounds' must be substituted for popular music; the agreeable noise emitted by hotel orchestra, gramophone, or wireless was not sufficiently isolated by 'listeners' to be appreciated as music, which implies some degree of form and organisation. It is easy enough to see why the attitude of so many owners of gramophone and especially wireless sets should have infuriated musicians such as Beecham and music critics such as Newman. The superseding of the wireless earphones by the loudspeaker was a considerable factor in encouraging people to switch on to whatever was being played, and leave it at that. That this could be considered heinous and immoral is understandable in its period; listeners at home were not expected to wear evening dress when Beethoven was on the wireless or gramophone, but they were relied on to prepare themselves mentally for a transcendental experience.

There was a schism between the suppliers and the experts, those who wanted to popularise classical music and those who wanted to preserve its integrity. Extraordinary efforts were made to bring classical music into everyday life, one of the most ludicrous examples being a concert at the Usher Hall, Edinburgh, sponsored by the Trades Union Congress to present music to illustrate the principles of trades unionism. A march by Franz von Blon, 'Sounds of peace', 'ushered in 100 per cent of Trades Unionism', the overture to Edward German's *Much Ado About Nothing* was 'illustrative of Baldwin's anti-Trades Union or Blacklegs' Charter Act, if the workers act together'. The overture to *Rienzi* typified 'the revolt of the people against oppression, just as the Trades Union Congress has to do now', while that old war-horse, Mendelssohn's 'Hebrides' overture had a programme note that threw new light on Mendelssohn's social attitudes: 'In this piece you can almost hear the waves dashing on the rocks and being broken up, as you will shortly see in the case of the attackers of Trades Unionism, with the resulting calm.' The concert was enthusiastically received. But such irrelevant tie-ups were no worse than those of newspaper writers reading into works hidden meanings.

A great opportunity was given to popularisers by the Beethoven centenary of 1927, as well as to musicologists who used the chance to put forward views that vie with those of the popularisers in improbability, and the intelligentsia to whom

Sir Henry Wood, who brought good music to the masses

Beethoven was old hat and who delighted in saying how much they detested his music. Howlers were promulgated by the hundred. A radio announcer said that Beethoven improvised his 'Moonlight' sonata for a blind girl; the same sonata, stated the *Musical Courier*, was written by Beethoven in his sleep.

Schoolchildren were asked to write essays on the subject. One ten-year-old boy wrote: 'Beethoven was a compositor. He was fond of music and of great poverty, so he made gramerphone records for a living and died poor. They sent him a hundred pounds to make him die happy, saying with his fleeting breath, "God bless them good fellows in London." ' A schoolgirl wrote: 'Beethoven wrote some funny music about Kate knocking at the door. He was deaf, and could not hear her, so she went on knocking all through the piece.'

So are the mighty fallen when their effusions are bandied about like pieces of merchandise. Perhaps fortuitously, a long article, 'For the people', by the American musicologist Alexander Fried came out in a musical quarterly:

> In our present society and culture, the art must automatically be harmed in proportion as popularisation is successful. To compete in catching skilfully-sought public interest, music must posture and gesticulate in antics such as those which make our newspapers and movies abominable. Some branches of the art, it is true, have greater potential showmanship than others. The mere co-operation of a hundred musicians in an orchestra is sufficiently spectacular to interest a fairly large group of our population—perhaps as much as five per cent.

The dilemma of the Frieds was that good music had to pay its way. Cheap jibes at the autocratic attitude of the BBC were all very well, but the BBC had taken the place of the patrons of the past responsible for the work of Haydn, Mozart, and even Wagner. With Chappell's refusing to carry on the Promenade Concerts, what would have happened had the BBC not stepped in? And what would the standard of the music have been if the Promenade Concerts had been run by an impresario intent only on making a profit?

*Opera for the many was tried out at the Surrey Theatre
and at the Old Vic, courageous attempts that never
truly succeeded* (Wonderful London)

A distinction must be made between the popular and the
fashionable; and popularity could be relative. Agreed that
Promenade Concerts were popular, but in comparison with
what? Only with ordinary symphony concerts. New British
operas such as *Romeo and Juliet* by Barkworth or *Excalibur* by
Colin McAlpin, names that mean nothing today, were *said* to be
popular when put on at the Surrey Theatre by the Fairbairn-Miln
Opera Company. 'The future is very promising for this experi-
ment,' wrote an anonymous correspondent in a weekly paper,
'for support has not been lacking by the public.' The Bishop of
Woolwich paid a visit and spoke warmly of the company's
good work, and encouragement was given by the mayor of the
borough. But with fringe opera, popularity could mean that the

theatre was more than half full or at worst not actually empty.

It is a matter of opinion whether Covent Garden opera was fashionable or popular, and certainly there were massive queues for the cheaper seats. Adulation of prima donnas was a long-held tradition, and for many devotees of the form the music was relatively unimportant. There was a good deal of snobbery connected with opera-going, and in 1927 the newspaper columnist Lady Eleanor Smith complained that 'nowadays people come to the opera dressed as for the theatre leaving their jewels behind them. It is rather sad'.

Compton Mackenzie came out with an attack on opera: 'We may admit that the English people do not support opera. But why should they be blackguarded for that? Operas, with very few exceptions, provide a prehistoric kind of entertainment, and the English failure to support them may be really a mark of civilisation.'

English music critics were severe on operatic artists, and Sir Henry Wood thought that the standard of singing was going steadily down. Sopranos lacked clearness and agility, contraltos

Queues outside Covent Garden waiting for the doors to open seem to indicate that opera was popular, not merely fashionable
(Wonderful London)

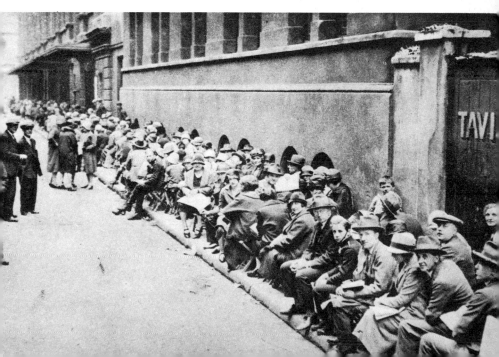

seemed to love gloom and stodginess, tenors were tight and throaty, and basses tended to the 'heavy, scoopy, lugubrious, and funeral-toned'. The big names of the times preferred to read what journalists wrote of them rather than critics. Thus James Douglas of Chaliapin:

> Odd it was to watch the fire of personality leaping out of this sexagenarian . . . Something in the mind of the singer changed the fiery mask of his face and the movements of his hands into a living outline of his thoughts and emotions. His flesh and his bones painted pictures in the air. His skin meditated.

The music critics were less flowery, and Chaliapin retaliated, laying waste all about him: 'England and America are games-mad; they will produce a future generation of enormous muscles and small brains.' And that was that, as far as he was concerned; countries that did not fully appreciate him deserved no better. There was criticism not only of performances by operatic stars, but of the ceremony that surrounded them and what was called the bouquet business. The wreath was even worse than the bunch of flowers. In 1923 the editor of the *Musical Times* commented: 'There is point in a wreath that may be worn on the head, the place where the wreath ought to go, but an affair like a cart-wheel suggests either a head abnormally swollen (even for a soloist) or use as a girdle for a 70-in. waist.' There were few who reacted in the manner of Sir Thomas Beecham when conducting ballet; he nonchalantly left the stage bowling a wreath off like a child's hoop.

Despite the great expense of putting on opera, there was no shortage of candidates; British composers were still intent on writing operas, and British opera houses put them on. In the nineteenth century many operatic ventures had come to grief on British opera, including the opera house in Cambridge Circus which foundered on the native product and was turned into the Palace Theatre of Varieties. Many of the operatic composers of the 1920s are now little known, if at all—Gatty, Somerville, Rootham, de Lara, Napier Miles and Bryson.

Rutland Boughton, whose The Immortal Hour
*was fashionable enough to be considered truly
popular* (*Lambert*)

There were operas that were fashionable often because they
were staged in picturesque surroundings, such as Rutland
Boughton's cult opera *The Immortal Hour* staged at Glastonbury.
There were composers who were supported for non-musical
reasons—Ethel Smyth by ex-Suffragettes.

Avant garde music was fashionable, but could be produced only
at small exclusive halls with high admission charges. Despite the
reputation of the pre-BBC Promenade Concerts for putting on
advanced music, such as Prokofiev's First Piano Concerto in
1920, Bartok's Rhapsody in 1921, and Bliss's Colour Symphony
in 1923, many of the prided first performances related to English
music that could have been classified in gramophone catalogues
or on the wireless as 'light orchestral'.

Some of the small-hall concerts drew audiences because of
their novelty value. Such concerts offered scope for the humorists
of the 1920s, and Harry Trevor, a knockabout journalist, found
them worth a couple of thousand words under a heading 'The
Music of To-morrow'.

'Hurrah!' said the callow youth with the fluid eyes. 'Firman Barewski (the fellow who wrote those beastly popular tunes) has got six months solitary Stravinsky. And a good job, too,' he added savagely, 'I'd have given him a year's Hullaballo.'

The Abolition of Melody Act had been passed, and tune-writing was an indictable offence. The State had nationalised the Arts along with the Railways and the Mines (Trevor was right there anyway), Wagner, Schumann, Schubert and the three Bs were strictly rationed, and the Minister of Fine Arts had 'inserted a clause in the new Bill permitting an example of each to be played once a week, provided the applicant was in possession of the necessary coupons'.

The leading composers of Trevor's nightmare were Cursedin, the Kalmuk; Pimpi, the young Italian; Nancy, the Frenchman; and Pandemonium, the Bashi-Bazouk.

Marvellous fellow, Cursedin. What we call an eliminist. Scores crossways—like a crab. He has abolished tonality, rhythm, and cosmic sounds generally. For him, music has passed far beyond the regions of the metaphysical, the psychological, and the philosophical . . .

Not so far off the mark, we may think, but novelty concerts depended for their success on whether they were in tune with current vogues or included cult figures in their *dramatis personae*. The most typical of these 'happenings' was the Sitwell/Walton *Façade*, poems spoken through a form of megaphone set in a screen specially painted by Frank Dobson and accompanied by Walton's music, which parodied many of the popular styles of the time such as the fox-trot and the tango. No participant was seen by the audience, and after the entertainment had been tried out privately—at which the clarinet-player had enquired during a pause in the music, 'Excuse me, Mr. Walton, has a clarinet player ever done you an injury?'—it was put on at the Aeolian Hall in June 1923, receiving sufficient abuse at the hands of the popular press and the establishment for it to be performed several times in the next few years for the enthusiastic supporters of modishness.

Reviling only increased the appetite for *Façade*, labelled 'Drivel they paid to hear' in one daily paper, with the exhortation that 'surely it is time this sort of thing were stopped'. Noel Coward made himself a hero to all right-minded people by walking out on it. When Arnold Bennett went to a performance of it in 1926 he was more interested in the audience than the entertainment: 'Crowds of people, snobs, highbrows, lowbrows, critics and artists and decent folk.'

The perspicacious who looked at *Façade* and similar phenomena realised that anything could be made a popular success if there was sufficient publicity. The arch revival of Victorian music hall at the Players' Theatre, sponsored by Elsa Lanchester, was another example of the *Façade* species. This, too, was a success among the hangers-on of show-biz. Simple snobbishness had a part to play in keeping such things alive, and popularity in these contexts had nothing to do with the content of the work. In the final analysis, the audience who attended the Aeolian Hall in 1923 were activated like dance bands, revue promoters, and the producers of songs for the mass market, programmed to that intensely twenties preoccupation—the quest for novelty.

SELECT BIBLIOGRAPHY

Agate, James. *Immoment Toys* (1945)

Bacharach, A. L. *British Music of Our Time* (1946)

Booth, J. B. *The Days We Knew* (1943)

Boulton, David. *Jazz in Britain* (1968)

Felstead, S. Theodore. *Stars Who Made the Halls* (1946)

Foss, Hubert, and Godwin, Noel. *London Symphony* (1954)

Fuld, James J. *Book of World Famous Music* (1966)

Gaisberg, F. W. *Music on Record* (1946)

Gammond, Peter. *Your Own, Your Very Own* (1971)

Gammond, Peter, and Clayton, Peter. *Guide to Popular Music* (1960)

Gelatt, R. *The Fabulous Phonograph* (1956)

Harris, Rex. *Jazz* (1952)

Howes, Frank. *English Musical Renaissance* (1966)

——. *Folk Music of Britain* (1969)

Hughes, Gervase. *Composers of Operetta* (1962)

Lambert, Constant. *Music Ho!* (1934)

Lee, Edward. *Music of the People* (1970)

Lloyd, A. L. *Folk Song in England* (1967)

London, Kurt. *Film Music* (1936)

Lubbock, Mark. *Complete Book of Light Opera* (1962)

Mackenzie, Compton. *My Record of Music* (1955)

Mackerness, E. D. *Social History of English Music* (1964)

Mackinlay, Sterling. *Origin and Development of Light Opera* (1928)

MacQueen Pope, W. *The Melodies Linger On* (1951)

Mander, Raymond, and Mitchenson, Joe. *British Music Hall* (1965)

——. *Musical Comedy* (1969)

——. *Revue* (1971)

Mendl, R. W. S. *The Appeal of Jazz* (1927)

Nettel, Reginald. *Sing a Song of England* (1954)

——. *Seven Centuries of Popular Song* (1956)

Orde-Hume, Arthur. *The Player Piano* (1970)

Pulling, Christopher. *They Were Singing* (1952)

Scholes, Percy A. *Oxford Companion to Music* (1938)

——. *Mirror of Music 1844–1944* (1947)

Short, Ernest. *Fifty Years of Vaudeville* (1946)

Short, Ernest, and Compton-Rickett, A. *Ring Up the Curtain* (1938)

Weatherly, Fred. *Piano and Gown* (nd)

White, Eric. *The Rise of Opera in England* (1951)

Willson Disher, M. *Winkles and Champagne* (1938)

——. *Fairs, Circuses and Music Halls* (1942)

Young, Percy M. *The Musical Tradition* (1962)

Newspapers, Periodicals and Magazines

Daily Express

Daily Herald

Daily Mail

Daily Telegraph

Dancing Times

Era

Gramophone

Ideal Home

John o' London's Weekly

Melody Maker

Monthly Musical Record

Musical News

Musical Opinion

Musical Standard

Musical Times

Musical World

Music Trades Record

The Observer

Punch

Strand Magazine

Talking Machine News

Tatler

The Times

INDEX